D1520887

BIRDS OF SORROW

Notes from a River Junction in Northern New Mexico

TOM IRELAND

ZEPHYR PRESS

The names of some people in *Birds of Sorrow* have been changed.

"Dog Days" was originally published in Blair & Ketchum's *Country Journal*
magazine, January 1980, © Cowles Magazines, Inc. "Shooting the Well" (under
the title "Trouble-Shooting the Well") was originally published in *Country
Journal* magazine, April 1988, © Cowles Magazines, Inc. "The Great Blue
Heron" and "Perils Not Insured Against" appeared in *Century*. "The House and
Its Inhabitants" appeared in *Resiembra*.

Color woodblock prints by Angie Coleman are
reproduced with permission of the artist.

Map by Charles Bahne

Design by Ed Hogan

ISBN 0-939010-19-4 (PBK)
Library of Congress Catalogue Card No. 91-65949

ZEPHYR PRESS
13 Robinson Street
Somerville, Massachusetts 02145, U.S.A.

You cannot prevent the birds of sorrow from flying over your head, but you can prevent them from building nests in your hair.

— Malcolm Lowry, *October Ferry to Gabriola*

CONTENTS

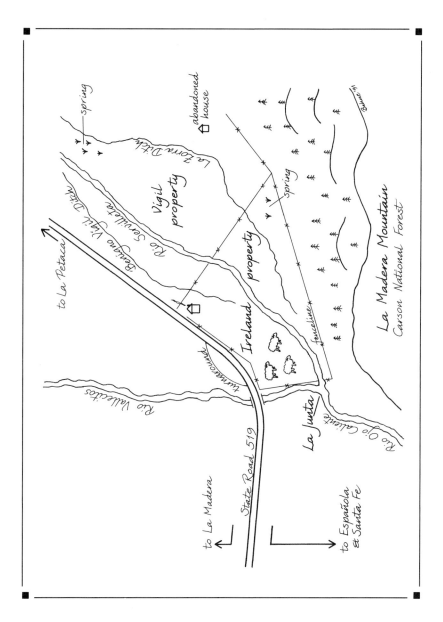

JESÚS, I'LL BE BACK

Jorge Luis Borges died last week. Once in New York nearly twenty years ago, I parked my taxicab on the street when I was supposed to be on duty and sat in a cold auditorium with a lot of other people to hear the great man of letters speak. He spoke of his blindness and the opportunity it had given him to read again, in memory, all the books he had ever read. He also read a poem about being home in Buenos Aires and missing Cambridge, Massachusetts, where he had taught — not so much that he loved Cambridge, but he loved the memory of being there and feeling homesick for Buenos Aires.

The same kind of nostalgia took me back to La Junta not too long ago. I wouldn't ever want to live there again. At the end of that last, miserable winter after my father died and my marriage ended, with all belongings piled high in one gorgeous dustbowl pickup load, I was glad to be leaving. On the front door, I left a message for the local state patrolman, a lame attempt to keep burglars out of the house: JESUS, I'LL BE BACK IN TEN MINUTES.

Three years later the old Ford pickup, belonging to the irredeemable past, had been traded in on a new Toyota. The house and property had been sold, and even though I still held the mortgage, sold a second time. The latest owner intended to split the place in two, keep most of the land for himself, and sell the house and one acre. It had been one property ever since it was first deeded, never part of something bigger, and unlike most of the farmland around there, never divided among heirs. In my vision of La Junta, the other side of the river was to remain permanently

[11]

undeveloped, a retirement home for coyotes. But this owner was not only talking about putting in a road and building another house over there, he wanted to dig ponds along the river and raise catfish for money. Catfish, in the hills of northern New Mexico! La Junta would be changed forever if that happened, losing the special qualities that brought me there in the first place: its quiet and separateness; the way that the river junction, the fields, and the mountain, although close to a paved road, felt miles away from traffic; the sense it had always given me of being in a small but complete and indivisible world.

Of course, none of this was any of my business, and I knew that by going back I was only letting myself in for disappointment. I knew that the whole adventure of buying property, building a house, raising livestock, and faithfully observing the life of the river junction had been just that, an adventure, and that this one had already come to an end. There was no hope of patching up my memories of the place, no forgiveness for having abandoned it to strangers. But I went anyway, mostly out of a conviction that before I could move ahead, I had to put that time and place behind me.

It had rained the night before, and the country was shining. The landscape had ripened over the years and become more interesting than I remembered it. Each new stretch of road, each speed zone, was inhabited by stories. The hanging tree, a gnarled cottonwood, with its single horizontal limb. Or the place where truckers were always losing their loads: you would be driving home from work and come around the bend when suddenly the whole world would be littered with forty-foot joints of white plastic irrigation pipe cast over the highway like pickup sticks, the jackknifed truck lying on its side in the arroyo.

About a mile and a half north of Ojo Caliente, the river leaves State Highway 285 and swings west into the hills, a region known to those who live there as *el quinto carajo*: the fifth, the quintessential sonofabitch, or not quite so literally, a very hard place to get along in. Formerly Colomex, now Petrolane, the gas company sits at the top of the hill where you turn for La Madera, white propane bottles of various sizes (papa bomb, mama bomb, little baby bomb) impounded behind a cyclone fence. A few years ago the state archaeological crew did some test digs close by on a prehistoric pueblo that lay buried in the path of highway improvements. Besides the usual potsherds, projectile points, and bone awls, they found the remains of two infants, but were unable to say what had killed them — birth, disease, starvation, or maybe the parents, too hungry themselves to provide for more.

There was a more recent Indian village near the turnoff once, according to a Vallecitos man. How long ago he couldn't say, he'd heard this story from his father, but for sure within historical times. One of the men of the village had a new bow he was especially proud of. A visitor bet him he couldn't shoot an arrow from there to the river. The arrow fell short, accidentally hitting a woman from the village who was hidden from view in the trees. The story didn't say what she had been doing down there, fetching water or meeting a lover, or what relation she was to the man who shot the arrow, or how things changed between them after that. The arrow lodged in her calf: as specific and unquestionable a detail as Achilles's heel. Hysterical, she ran along the river with the arrow sticking out of her leg until the people heard her screams. They ran after her and caught her, pinned her to the ground to get the arrow out, then doctored her with "some plants that were

[13]

growing there." No historical marker marks the spot.

At the gas company, Jake Honeycutt, a man of many keys, made brief statements on the weather while you were waiting for your gas bottle to fill. "Don't care for this wind." Those who turn there aren't just passing through. The road doesn't go anywhere but into the mountains, turning to gravel, then dirt, then driveways and logging tracks. The nature of the road changes drastically after the turn, along with the nature of the people driving over it. They wave, even if you have been away for three years. Instead of a number, the road takes the name of wherever you happen to be going. It dips down and through a wide, sandy arroyo. Parts of unnameable machineries, as if shot or fallen from atmospheric heights, stick up out of the sand. The arroyo has no culverts. Nothing grows in it, and it gathers a considerable head of water in a summer cloudburst. Traffic has to stop once in a while to let the flood go by, and when it has, the road will be buried under several inches of sparkling pink sand until the highway department comes to blade it off.

The road follows the old railroad bed in places, but what hasn't been paved over has been mostly washed away, dissolved into the surrounding contours. It curves the way a road ought to curve in rough country, going around obstacles instead of through them. The yellow sign with the curvy arrow warns that the road is about to stop being straight, but it isn't the old sign, which has long since been shot to pieces or run down, as this one will be too, keeping the sign-making factory in Ojo Caliente in business. People like to drive on the wrong side of the road going through these curves, skirting Mesa Vista, home of the Trojans. ("Their horses shone like the rays of the sun, terribly.") When traveling in opposite directions and passing one another on the highway, a local family had the custom of switching lanes at the last moment so that each car would pass the other on the left. It was their trademark, like a fraternity handshake. One day, one of the cars failed to make the switch, they met head on, and people died in the wreck.

Across the first bridge, at La Cueva, the valley widens. Holes and cavities of all sizes, the homes of porcupines and owls, riddle the cliff face across a pasture to the east. Once in a dream, I was chased by a great white bear through the sunlit rooms and passageways of these cliffs, and thinking I had escaped, came face to face with an even bigger white bear, the other one's mother, the unbenign god of the labyrinth. That house on the left, sitting above another killer curve, once housed an authority on the bird life of South Africa. On the right, the relic of a hippy commune, one of few such surviving that sprouted in northern New Mexico twenty years ago, with outlandish peaked dwellings and a birdhouse in the same architectural style, hanging from a dead cottonwood next to a hot spring. In an alkaline wash, where sandpipers wade in stagnant pools, the heavenly tamarisk puts out its cotton-candy-pink blossoms. Flanking hillsides erode into deep crevasses (one can stand in them, watch clouds move across that slash of blue sky, and feel the earth turn). Next there's a large white house with red trim, at different times the home of earnest leftists; a gentle chiropractor, who had retired but whose patients followed him there from the ends of the earth; and a man of visions, an Ojibway Indian, who once saw a ghost farmer down in the field and took it as a sign that he was meant to plant wheat there. A little further on, just before town, lives a man who had been a beautician until someone in town died a horrible death and by no means or agent could be made to look even vaguely human again until he came to the rescue, using tricks of the beauty trade combined with a professional knowledge of meatcutting, thus starting yet another career as a mortician, specializing in miraculous and lifelike regenerations.

What was once my place lies at the junction of two mountain streams, immediately after you cross the bridge on the road to La Petaca ("the suitcase"). As long as anyone living can remember, La Petaca has been where the outlaws lived, and presumably, where they knew the law would not follow them. It could be "the suitcase" because the valley is small and hemmed in by hills, or because so many of the outsiders who tried to settle there have been forced to pack up and move on in a hurry.

I parked across the road from the house at what we always called "the turnaround," a piece of riverbank that probably went with the rest of the property at one time but got sliced off by the road, left unfenced, and through years of being used by anybody for whatever they pleased (washing the car, making backseat love) fell into the public domain. Only suspicious people parked at the turnaround, and it was a favorite place for parties. Before the house was built, I made the mistake of going over there at two o'clock in the morning to ask if they could please be a little quieter, my wife and I were trying to sleep. All of a sudden it got a whole lot quieter. About a dozen men were standing around a fire, and they were looking at me and not saying anything, unable to believe that anybody, least of all an unarmed gringo who had just materialized out of darkest midnight and on foot, besides, could be that dumb. When one of them slipped a load into his shotgun and pointed it at me, I understood that it was time to turn around and walk back to my side of the road.

Across the road from the turnaround I built a fence between the bridge and the existing fence corner, a distance of no more than thirty feet, to keep cars from driving down the embankment to the river junction. It had to be rebuilt every few months, whenever someone drove over it or cut the wire. The owner before me had wanted to keep it open to the public for "picnics." He lived in Albuquerque, two hours away, so it was easy enough for him to be generous. No, this was to be a bird sanctuary. If cars could be kept off the bank long enough for the weeds to come up — cottonwood, willow, tamarisk, and lovers of bulldozed ground like yellow clover and mullen — then the birds would have cover. And if I ever saved up enough money to buy a pair of binoculars, I might even be able to sit and birdwatch from my front yard.

The fence had fallen to pieces again. A broken cedar fencepost. A vicious loop of barbed wire hidden among last year's Russian thistles, mining the only approach to the junction. But the public seemed to have gotten the idea. Unlike the turnaround, its orphan cousin across the road, the river junction was coming back nicely. The highway department had channeled the river, a measure to keep the bridge from getting washed out during storm runoff. Young willows were coming up through the levee of dredged river cobbles, cleaner than dinner plates, where you wouldn't think anything could find a place to grow. This, the very cottonwood from which I'd stolen a fledgling magpie out of its nest, had broken strangely halfway up the trunk. The top half had fallen across the fence and dragged it down to where the cows that sometimes ran loose along the river, and who had an uncanny talent for finding downed fences, could easily have stepped across. That would have to be fixed. The pasture looked run-down, and dozing under the cottonwoods across the Servilleta were two of the reasons for it: horses. The alfalfa was gone now, and even though the ground was still wet from the rain, it looked parched and sick.

It wouldn't have done any harm to go in the yard and take a look at the apple trees, the cherry, the yellow roses and the pink hedge roses, the Russian olive; to see if the hollyhocks and the horehound and the other perennials were still hanging on; if there were anything left of the raspberry patch; if bark beetles were still attacking the juniper tree. I would have liked to look closer to see how the mud plaster was holding up on the outside and whether the gable ends and the windows needed paint, if the grease trap were still trapping grease. The house had been burglarized time and again since we sold it, once by someone who ran a hose through a window and left it running in the living room, just for spite. So had the studio, where I had spent the last winter as caretaker, subservient to the new owner when he dropped in every now and then on vacation from Hollywood, California, wishing I had the courage to murder his dog, and finally deciding I'd had enough when he told me that my geese, the last farm animals on the place and about the only thing there I still found unfailingly beautiful, would have to be locked in the chicken pen. I could have broken in the bathroom window where I had broken in so many times before when the keys were locked in the house, delicately prying the window stop away from but not off the frame, just enough to slip a spoon handle under the latch and step into the cast-iron bathtub. (Would it still be there, or had it been torn out and replaced by some godawful fiberglass shower stall?) I would have liked to walk through the house remembering the work of six years I put in there, a handbuilt house if there had ever been one,

and all the ignorance and unintentional grace that would continue to show through no matter how many times it changed hands. The living room with its floor of cracked mud, replaced during my years of absence by a wooden floor so that now the ceiling beams, peeled logs of fir and spruce, would be lower overhead, in a room that had a low ceiling to begin with. The staircase, marvel of book-learned engineering, the width of its treads actually in correct ratio to the width of its risers. And the upstairs, which was necessary because the country houses of my childhood, one in Connecticut and one in Delaware, had had them, and because I had grown up in the one dimension of a city apartment. Upstairs, the white walls; the single yellowing skylight on the north because Molly, my wife, was an artist and north light was artist's light; the floor that in its last life had been a basketball court and that had been paced those many nights when Hannah, my daughter, woke barking with the croup and sometimes barely able to breathe; and at the east end, the French doors from which I had seen my neighbor's haystack, enough hay for a hundred cows for the winter, go up in a mountain of flame.

It was here, upstairs, where the chainsaw had been hidden in the crawl space under the eaves when the thieves broke in that last winter and took everything I had of much value — all the tools that had built the house, and the hardest loss of all, my birding binoculars, paid for with small bills and loose change saved in a coffee can. I should have known something like that would happen. Only the Ford had been parked outside since the fall, and when it was gone, it was obvious to them, as it was to me now, that nobody was home. I returned late one night from town to find a pane of glass in the front door broken, the door wide open, but the rest of the house in perfect order, nothing broken, nothing left thrown on the floor. Strangely, they hadn't taken the rifles — according to Jesús, usually the first thing to be taken, even before money and liquor. But they found the chainsaw in its hiding place under the eaves, a space Hannah used to make me check for monsters before she would go to sleep. They took the last can of beer out of the refrigerator. And they found the binoculars in the top drawer of the dresser, under the socks. Losing them had been to lose what little remained of my reason for being there.

I stood at the turnaround for a while with the broken beer bottles, the tire tracks and the charred ring of stones from the last party, trying to decide whether or not to cross the road and climb over the fence for a closer look. The new owner probably would not have minded. Hadn't he written a letter praising everything we'd done, saying how much he appreciated all the care and foresight that had gone into it?

The roof was starting to get a little rusty, but it wasn't a bad roof, considering it was the first I'd ever framed. I'd tacked a juniper bough to the ridge rafter when the framing was done, an old-world blessing, and that must have been what kept the weather out. The front gate was locked, and a large white freezer with the word "ice" in red, the kind they have in supermarkets, stood by the back door: catfish? In back, by the pumphouse, someone had taken the sheepwire off its posts. A tractor had pushed the bank out and away from the house, I could see the tread marks, and the peninsula of gray dirt pointing towards the river that looked like the beginnings of a road. If they planned on building on the other side, they would have to build a bridge to cross the river, and it would have to be strong enough for trucks. The road would have to cross irrigated pasture, and it was always wet on that end when the ditch was running. They would always be getting stuck. The house would go above the ditch, in among the scrub oaks and the few red junipers that had not been taken for posts. Others had tried before and given up. An adobe ranchhouse had already been standing on the neighbor's side of the fence for forty years with nobody living in it except a pair of summering sparrowhawks and an occasional flicker, not worth the trouble it took to get to it.

But the problems belonged to someone else now. As much as I would have liked to cross the road and take a closer look, all the looking I had left to do would be from a distance — remembering how difficult that life was, how passionately we had courted difficulty, and at the last, how badly I wanted to leave. From where I stood, maybe I could discover something about it that for all my careful looking I had missed before. Like that splash of deciduous green high up on the mountain, holding its own against the junipers and piñons. A spring.

THE TWO-HEADED CALF

It's still standing there in the La Madera post office, past the mug-shots, on top of the glass display case with the party dresses. It was born that way, with two heads. They found it dead the next day, had it stuffed and mounted, and took a few snapshots: the two-headed calf with Delio, the postmaster; the two-headed calf alone, standing on the hood of a car. Below it, a color press photograph of a thoroughbred race horse has been taped to the display case: A Swift Dancer in the winner's circle at a bigtime Arizona racetrack. A caption identifies the jockey as Z. Chacon of La Madera, New Mexico.

Delio showed me the two-headed calf the first time I ever visited the post office, when I went to apply for a mailbox. He probably showed it to anybody new as a way of getting acquainted. You couldn't very well see it and not have something to say. It was April, and the barn swallows had not yet returned from the tropics to resume their depredations on the post office, building their mud nests between the porch rafters and spattering the concrete walk. Year after year, Delio knocked the nests down with a broom, but the swallows kept coming back.

The sign outside the post office reads "La Madera Mercantile: General Merchandise." They sell bread, lunch meat, and soda pop, but not much of anything, and almost everybody calls it *el correo* — the post office. Sometimes you still hear it called *la estafeta*," also a post office, but what a post office used to be — a way station, a place to get off your horse and rest a while. Many of the people who get their mail there live close enough to walk, within the quarter-mile strip of road and houses that is the town of La Madera, beginning at the south end with what used to be the school and ending on the north with the turnoff to what used to be the dump. The school has been boarded up, the dump filled in: now the garbage and the children are driven miles to their respective destinations.

The town ("village" is too precious for La Madera) still looks like what it was sixty years ago — a sawmill town. The name means "lumber." The Denver and Rio Grande Railroad built a narrow-gauge spur to La Madera in 1914 to haul out lumber (and later, vegetable packing crates) for Hallock & Howard, the company that owned the mill. The large, nearly windowless building that now houses the post office and the mercantile were probably part of the milling operation to begin with — maybe a warehouse with a loading dock to the tracks on the downhill side, where the irrigation ditch runs now. The building belongs to some much grander, more ambitious enterprise than delivering the mail. In the back room, even bigger and emptier than the room the customer sees, the scale that was once used to weigh ore from nearby mica mines — Little Julia, Sunnyside, Big Bug — has never been moved. Mica is one of the few things besides lumber that La Madera was ever known for. They have dances and wedding receptions in the back. The town's entire population, with in-laws thrown in for good measure, doesn't come close to filling it. For years, the federal government has been trying to close the post office because it handles so little mail, but like the swallows, it refuses to be eliminated.

The timber played out during the depression and the railroad pulled up its tracks. They left the railroad ties, though, and people took them home and made things out of them — barns and chicken sheds, even houses — laying them up in courses with mud in between and sometimes plastering them over. A chicken house made of railroad ties, warm in winter and cool in summer, means eggs all year long.

La Madera has two stores and two gas pumps, one more of each than it needs. The town doesn't seem to be getting any bigger, though a new house went up a few years ago — a son building across the road from his father, close enough for them to stand in their doorways and have a conversation without shouting. And not just a trailer house, either, but a real house on a foundation of La Madera river rock that can't be jacked up and moved to some faraway heathen country at a moment's notice — a house meant to stay and last. Other houses have gone up in the neighborhood, but not within the protective and sometimes stifling close bounds of the pueblo. These houses, crammed together on the ditch bank and scattered on the hillside across the road, belong in a way that other houses and people, however close by and however closely related, never will.

From the outside, La Madera probably does not look too different from the way it looked in 1930 when the mill folded, a town built for an urgent, exhaustible, commercial purpose — a shanty town, the kind that might once have been occupied almost exclusively by unshaven men in boots. If it had been as picturesque as the logging camps of California or the Northwest, someone might have photographed all one hundred working inhabitants standing in front of the Hallock & Howard office, hands in pockets, a pipe here and there, many of them ragged, and not a smile in the crowd.

Years before I moved to La Madera, in country east of there, some of us were building a hogan. It was December. We froze at night in a tipi and ate white bread and grease soup in a tarpaper shack with a dirt floor, trying to get the roof on before the first big snow. Like settlers. One afternoon, a visitor came and asked who had designed the hogan. "Nobody designed it," he was told, "we just built it." Most of La Madera's like that — just built, and mainly with the idea of getting into something with four walls and a roof before the first big snow. It was built by people who had not done much building before and intended to do as little of it as possible after. But unlike houses built by builders for other people to live in — the square and plumb kind, the kind that get designed — these houses had the commitment of the builders to live in them, no matter what the inconveniences, a residing commitment long after the builders have passed on.

Rough houses, but rough only on the outside. Within, each is a shrine, with a cleanliness and order you never could have guessed from the patched-over, man-handled outsides. Inside, where the woman arranges things to her liking, and where the man is often treated more as a guest than a resident — someone permitted to sit in that chair, provided he's washed, but not to say where it will go — inside that makeshift stack of splintery railroad ties that looks as if it might be intending to slide off the hill one day soon, all's queenly ceremony. The kitchen stove is so white that it hurts to behold it. Pictures of young men in uniform, pastel maidens, and gentle couples adorn the mantlepiece. And above it, protecting and perpetuating all, the Virgin of Guadalupe, La Madera's patroness. Allowing that in stories told in this town, as they are told in towns everywhere in the world, supernatural beings are always turning up on people's doorsteps disguised as beggars, the stranger in that house will be treated, if not with the loving familiarity of family, with the respect that would be afforded to a god.

Once I was coming back to New Mexico on the train from Chicago. We passed through a place very much like La Madera — a few ruined adobes by the side of the tracks that nobody lived in any more; the usual galleries of dead cars; the church, very pink, like La Madera's church; a goat in somebody's front yard, gnawing on a tree that had been stripped clean ages ago. A woman across the aisle was looking out the window, shaking her head. To nobody in particular, she said, "What in the world do these people do?"

At first I felt offended by the remark, the pity and condescension that it implied. Her glimpse of the place from a rolling train had already told her everything she wanted to know about it, that there were not any movie houses or industrial parks, so there was obviously nothing to do. But I too had a certain investment in her image of small-town life as isolated and backward. I prized the special strangeness of my chosen place, if not the probability that I would never be anything but an *afuero* (outsider) there; and so, doubly isolated. In fact, I felt very protective of that strangeness. I did not want it to get even a hair less strange, compromised in any way by what I perceived as the killing normalcy of the world outside, where there's always something to do.

Petaca Joe the hitchhiker was there that day I first visited the post office, so he holds the place in memory reserved for the first person met and the first kindness shown. He introduced himself with ceremony worthy of a knight errant, saying all of his names and the names of all his relations, and bought me a strawberry soda. Delio signed me up for a box, then motioned confidentially for me to come around to the side where people picked up their packages. There in the dimness, high overhead on top of the display case, was the two-headed calf.

It stood rigidly at attention, the way they make animals stand for judging at a show, and it was leaning forward, as if to keep from hitting one or both heads on the ceiling. Apart from having two heads, the calf seemed perfectly normal. The heads were small, and pointier than the heads of most white-faced calves; but they were complete, with the right number of ears, eyes, noses, and mouths, and nearly the same size. There was no main head, and no horrible, half-formed afterthought. No distress or embarrassment in the expression of either face. A hint of surprise, maybe, but nothing to suggest it deserved any better.

The calf had been born during an extremely cold night in November, and might have frozen. Sometimes a newborn will go numb with the shock of freezing cold air and not be able to rise and take its mother's milk. The calf might have stuck to the frozen ground the way a wet hand will stick to a tray of ice cubes; or it might have been born dead. Nobody knew because the birth happened at night and only the other cows witnessed it. They would have shown their usual interest, sauntering over in the early morning to take a look at the newborn out of curiosity and their sense of belonging to the community of birthgivers. And what about the mother? When she felt the heaviness slip away from her that morning and turned around to see what new thing life had presented, did she see a monster, or have the slightest notion that something wasn't the way it was supposed to be? Not likely. She just did what had to be done, licking the skin of wetness from the calf so it could breathe, first one nose, then the other, nudging it to stand.

I used to walk to town to get the mail. Our house stood clear across the other side of the river, only ten minutes by foot, but definitely separate in the local thinking. The west side of the river was town; everything east was wilderness. Perhaps only fifteen years earlier, before the bridge went in, you would have had to ford the river to get across. A La Madera woman told Molly that she and her husband had considered building their house where we had built ours, but decided the place was too isolated. They feared the desperadoes of La Petaca, just as earlier European settlers had feared Apaches and Comanches, and chose instead the safety of the La Madera side.

Half of the distance between our house and the post office, all the way across the bridge to the only intersection in town with a stop sign, was unlived in — a grazed field on the left, with borders of cockleburrs, sunflowers, and baby cottonwoods; and a planted field on the right, always well plowed, watered, and weeded. The Ortegas grew corn and chile there, and one year, a lovely crop of oats. There is great healing power in the sight of oats, the faintly blue color of their stems, the knack of each seedhead to hold a single, radiant drop of moisture after rain.

The windows of the old school building had been covered over with plywood and green corrugated fiberglass. The roof was painted metal. Former paint jobs (red and yellow) were weathering through the most recent one (green), which made it look like a painting of a roof. Not too long ago, if you had grown up in La Madera you got all the schooling you were going to get from kindergarten through twelfth grade in this one building, passing from one grade to the next without the happy illusion of getting somewhere that comes from changing rooms and teachers. Uvaldo sold beer out of a tiny white house with a barred window next door. He sat in there sometimes all day long, like a delicate, caged finch in his eyeglasses and straw hat, nested in the dark amid the shining stacks of Schlitz, Budweiser, and Coors. La Pasada, the other store besides the post office, got the liquor. The owners eventually barred off the glass front and installed an alarm system to stop break-ins. It didn't take the bad boys long to figure out they could set off the alarm by firing a very loud gun (shotguns worked best) in the middle of the night. I'd wake to gunfire, roll over, and go back to sleep, thinking, "All's well. They're shooting in La Madera."

On the corner, the white stucco house with the red trim tried to be a restaurant. They spray-painted the words "Mexican Food" on the side of the house in red and went into business. It lasted a few years. They served what some said was first-rate cooking and others said was puppy meat. Something dreadful always seemed to be happening on that corner. Once, a man was electrocuted when his girlfriend threw an electric heater into the bathtub with him. Directly across the road, in and around the turquoise house with the row of exotic-looking trees and that other oddity in La Madera, a lawn, everything was tidy and proper. This was Mr. Griego's house. The same kind of trees grew on the street in New York where I grew up, out of holes in the sidewalk, down the hill where the nuns lived. In every season, Mr. Griego's yard was tidier than most people's living rooms. His marvelous woodpile, stacked so soundly that anything larger than a chipmunk would have had a hard time finding a place to crawl in, was the closest thing in town to architecture.

Except for the pink church, with its bell tower and its bell, from there to the post office it was all houses and trailers. I would look at each of those houses and wonder what kind of life went on inside, if it were anything like mine or forever and incomprehensibly different. There was enough strangeness here to last a lifetime. The dogs didn't trust anybody on foot. Each yard had at least one dog, and at Olympia's, where a wash always hung over a sheepwire fence and the creeper vines alone seemed to be holding up the front porch, there were sometimes many dogs. They would hear me thinking about things that were none of my business, rise painfully from their sleep, and bark. I learned to put one hand on the ground, which in a language understood by dogs everywhere means you are picking up a rock.

After people left for distant jobs in the morning, cars came through town at long intervals — long enough for the dogs to fall asleep in the road. The mail came in about ten o'clock. Those who were richest in time, usually the oldest, sat on a wooden bench in back of the post office and talked. In summer, during pauses in their conversation, you could hear the barn swallows — those squeaking noises with the up-and-down intonations of speech, the small bursts of wings when they took flight.

The strangeness wore thin. In time, the dogs of La Madera hardly blinked at me when I walked into town for the mail, hoping for proof of my existence — something, no matter what, with my name on it. I stopped reaching for imaginary rocks. If time had already started to absorb me into the appearance and the custom of the place, I suppose more time could have finished the job. I could have become another one of those mirthless faces in the photograph, standing out in front of the company store and wondering what the photographer saw that was interesting enough to take a picture of.

LAW OF THE LAND

It rained and snowed that Easter week. In the wet everything showed its true color: the willows flamed, the chamisa by the road turned green. A solitary red-winged blackbird uttered a few half-hearted cries, as if it doubted the season.

It was all strange to me, coming most recently not from a far-off coast, but from a mere thirty miles to the east across a sagebrush plain which separated an old country from one that seemed older by far; as if the deep rift of the Rio Grande gorge in the middle of that plain posed an obstacle not only to travel but also to the passage of time. In migrating thirty miles I had abandoned a country and a century.

I felt this strangeness most acutely one Sunday morning after we bought the property in La Madera. Molly and I drove the back way through the mountains to see the land again, to see if it was what we had first seen, or if it had somehow changed now that it was officially ours. The dirt road (it was mud then, only the ruts kept us from sliding off) led down out of the hills through the village of La Petaca, a few adobe dwellings with tin roofs clustered near the church. The adult population of La Petaca stood in the churchyard. The black-shawled women were lined against one windowless wall of the church, facing the men, who made a knot in one corner of the churchyard. The men looked up as we drove by, the olive-gray faces tight, suspicious. I smiled and waved; then I saw the mound of dirt, the heap of plastic flowers, the short box of rough-sawn planks. They were burying a child.

I guessed from the faces in the churchyard that I was to be a stranger here for some time. There have been times since when I wished for nothing but the comfort of a New England home, the company of people more like myself, the nearness of kin; knowing all the time that if I had these things I would leave them and seek to be a stranger again.

So I found myself on that rainy Maundy Thursday arranging buckets and fruit jars to catch the leaks in the trailer where we would live until the house was built. Molly was staying with friends for a few days. I was waiting for the rain to stop so I could get to work on the house, but if I waited on the rain at the start of the job, I would probably be working in the snow at the end of it. The clouds lifted in the afternoon and I could see the frozen hilltops. My land lay at the base of La Madera Mountain at the junction of two rivers: Rio Vallecitos, still clear before the runoff had gotten well under way; and the chalky Rio Servilleta ("napkin river"), which ran through the middle of our place from north to south, where it joined the Vallecitos. They called our ten acres "La Junta" — the junction.

No one had lived at La Junta since Woodrow Wilson deeded it to Crisanta M. de Martínez and her heirs "to have and to hold in perpetuity." I was the first, the only human resident. That afternoon, between pulses of rain and snow, I broke ground for the foundation and wondered why none of the previous owners had built there. Was it the bulk of the mountain in the winter, blocking the morning sun? Too close to the rivers, and so, too many mosquitos in the summer? Was my soil too rocky and alkaline to grow anything, simply not worth the trouble? Were they afraid to build that far from the plaza because of the outlaws who rode down out of the hills from La Petaca? The town of La Madera, salvaged from a work camp of the twenties when they cut railroad ties from the tall timber and mined mica near La Petaca, sat on a hillside only a few hundred yards west of the confluence of the two rivers; yet I'd already been asked at the post office how the weather was at La Junta, as if my land were something apart.

Towards evening the sun dropped into a corridor between the clouds and the little valley was filled with pink light. I put down my shovel and stood under a juniper to witness the change. It was like being in an aquarium: immersed, the bare cottonwoods, the hillside, the vacant house across the river, the fenceposts, my own hands acquired a light of their own. The air filled with sugary spines of ice, and a rainbow appeared, its northern pole planted in the willows of the neighbor's cow pasture. I could see impossible distances in every direction — up the valley to La Zorra, down the crooked Vallecitos, up the *cañada* behind Vigil's store — as if I could see around corners. A dog barked behind me. An old woman stood there on the road with an army of dogs around her. Her long gray hair was streaked with white, and she had it tied at the end with purple ribbon. She wore basketball sneakers, red and green striped socks rolled below her knees, a gray woolen jumper over a red sweater. She was facing me and talking in Spanish, her arms held high over her head, the fingers spread, as if delivering an invocation. The dogs stood respectfully at her feet, hanging out their tongues. She looked not at me but through me, in the direction of the rainbow, her face twisted and girlish, the words delivered with her whole body. Then she walked on down the road towards La Zorra, the dogs trotting ahead and behind.

Marauding dogs woke me that night. Two or three of them

were barking in the vicinity of the abandoned adobe on the other side of the river. From what I had seen of the house, no one had lived there for many years. The realtor told me it was the town *morada*, a meeting place for a religious brotherhood, Hermandad de Nuestro Padre Jesús Nazareno. Important rituals took place during Holy Week, especially on Good Friday. Devotees believed the souls of departed *penitentes* took human form and fell into the ranks of the Holy Week processions.

The dogs continued to bark as if they had all the time in the world and no good reason to stop. I couldn't get back to sleep. I thought of going over there, but the river was too high. A log that I'd hauled from the Vallecitos sawmill for a footbridge had washed away with the melt. I lit a lantern and took down the Gideon's Bible that the previous owner of the trailer had left behind. I hardly ever read the Bible, but at that hour, alone, in a strange place, it seemed like the thing to do. I opened it at random, the way I'd seen my grandmother do it when I was a boy, and read the last psalm, number 150. "Let every thing that hath breath praise the Lord." The dogs kept barking.

When I woke on Good Friday morning I heard a tractor running in the distance, and I wondered what kind of man would work on this holy day, in those villages, observed even more fastidiously than Easter. It was snowing lightly. The dogs had gone home, or assumed some other form, and nothing moved near the morada. I went to the river with a bucket for water to wash the dishes, crossing the stony pasture below the ditch where we'd parked the trailer. The river was brown and on the rise. A pile of foam eddied in a hollow against the opposite bank. The muddy water I dipped into the bucket looked as if it had already done the dishes.

A backhoe crawled out of the swamp at a wide meander upstream and headed towards me in traveling gear. A round man wearing a cowboy hat sat at the controls, one hand on the wheel, the other holding a can of soda. Every time the backhoe hit a bump I could see daylight between him and his machine. He saw me and left the backhoe idling by the gate while we talked across the fence. His name was Joe Vigil, the owner of the property next to mine. His hat beaten down and curled to a point in front. He sprayed me with Skol when he spoke.

"You owe me fifty dollars. That is, if you want to use the water. The man who owned this property never paid me to clean the ditch. Five years he owned your place and never once did he pay or send someone to work. Five years, ten dollars a year, fifty dollars."

That was my welcome to La Madera. He drained his Pepsi and tossed the can on my side of the fence. I'd never heard about any fifty dollars. The purchase agreement read "all ditch dues etc. to be paid to date of closing . . . property clear of all liens and encumbrances save none."

I told him as much, that I'd bought the place free of debt, and that if he thought he had fifty dollars coming to him, he'd better take it up with Hal Shipton, the previous owner.

"Cheapton, that's what I call him," said Vigil.

I'd bought the property from Shipton, but I'd never met him, never even spoken to him on the phone. All I knew about him was that he ran cattle near Tres Piedras, and that he lived in Albuquerque.

"I like to stay on good terms with everybody, Arnold."

"Ireland."

"If you don't want to use the water, that's none of my business, but if you do, you have to pay me the fifty dollars. I just fixed the ditch with the backhoe. It would have taken you a week to do it with a shovel. Just pay me the fifty dollars, and you can have all the water you want. The ditch on the other side, now that's something different. We're going to clean it tomorrow morning. Everybody cleans his own part of it and then we all clean it from Gurule's up to the headgate. Ernie Gurule, he's in charge of that ditch, so you can take it up with him. But I can tell you right now," pointing a finger at me, "if you want to use the water on that side you owe us one hundred and thirty dollars for the tractor work we did two summers ago when that whole hillside collapsed. And you have to help us tomorrow. Eight o'clock, and bring some workers."

"I don't know anybody around here. How do you expect me to find any help by tomorrow?"

"I'm going to have three men working," said Vigil. "You have to supply equal labor."

He stomped off and remounted the backhoe. No talk of the weather, no questions about who I was or where I had come from or what I was doing there — not that I was sure I knew myself.

When the backhoe crossed the bridge to town, I took a shovel and climbed through the barbed wire to Vigil's side of the fence. The clouds were breaking behind the morada where the line of the mountain dropped to low hills. Cows had eaten the willows on his side down to sickly nubs. The ditch, choked with manure, weeds, and straw, ran along the edge of the pasture, then cut back towards the tangled river bank. On the water survey, they called it the Benigno Vigil ditch — Joe's father, I assumed, listed on the title abstract as the man who had owned La Junta before Shipton. Only the two fields, mine and Vigil's, were irrigated from this ditch, so the talk across the fence had been a meeting of the board. I felt exposed walking on the other man's land, a trespasser, though the water survey said I had every right to be there. Taking water from someone was no different from any other kind of stealing. I'd heard that in that country, when a man went to take the water without permission it was a good idea to carry a rifle.

The ditch led me onto a muddy bank between the river and a cattail swamp, an oxbow where beavers lived. Vigil had dammed the head of the ditch and pulled a stinking heap of black muck from it. I broke up the dam until it slumped under the weight of the river, and water broke into the ditch. I walked ahead of it, wanting to get out of there quickly and stand my own ground again. Cattle were drifting into the field from the river. A white-faced cow with a calf widened her stance when I passed, lowered her head menacingly, and took a few swaying steps backward.

I waited for the water on the terrace above the ditch where I had started trenches for the foundation of the house. An old man with a cane was leading a big red-roan mare across the bridge from town. There was another horse, an unhaltered colt that crowded against its mother and nuzzled its head over her neck to see what was on the other side. Stiff-necked, the old man walked in the middle of the pavement. I could see his eyes shifting when he got close, watching the road, and the colt, and me all at once. He turned into the driveway, lifted his cane in greeting, and tied the mare to a fencepost. The colt went to pulling weeds, and the old man stepped over to the edge of the bank where I was looking out for the water. He spoke Spanish, and smiled all the time. The world was a joke. He reminded me of an Indian man I knew: the cane; the twinkling, sunny demeanor; something oriental and female about him. His name was Celestino Montoya, and he wanted me to pasture his horses. When I tried to answer in Spanish, he shook his head. Hopeless.

"You rent?"

"No horses," I said. "Maybe cows, but not now. Maybe next winter, four or five cows."

He shook his head again.

"We no can talk. You drink?"

He took a flask of whiskey from a pocket inside his vest and shoved it at me. I took a drink.

"Good boy."

He took the bottle and drank.

"You see deer?"

"No, no deer, only tracks."

"Long time, no deer," he said sadly. "Long time, lotsa deer," pointing his cane across the river. "Lotsa meat. Too much cows now. No deer."

He put the whiskey back in his vest, and leaning on the cane with both hands, stared off into the hills across the river. A clutter of cow pads and rotten straw was inching down the ditch.

"Here comes the water," I said.

"Lotsa *pastura* this year, huh?"

The two of us watched the water come, so slowly that once I thought it had stopped moving altogether.

"You sell hay?"

"Maybe. Maybe I'll just feed it."

"You got cows?"

"No, not yet. Looks like he's got all the cows." I motioned to Vigil's herd.

"Okay, boy. Maybe Gurule." He lifted his cane again, a parting salute, and untied the roan. On the road the colt walked sideways behind his mother, looking back spooky-eyed to see where he had been.

The water ran through a rose bramble at the fence line and into a willow thicket. I heard a sucking noise, as if someone were draining a bathtub. The willows whipped my face when I crawled into the thicket. What little water had come that far was running into a gopher hole in the bottom of the ditch. I crammed a rock into the hole. It disappeared into the maelstrom. I found a bigger rock and jumped on it until it sealed the leak. Grudgingly, the water trickled along the ditch, rounded the bank, and made a little pool in the field, about enough for a bird bath. But I'd made my point.

That evening I drove to Ojo Caliente to call Hal Shipton. He informed me that the Benigno Vigil ditch had been opened for the sole purpose of irrigating my pasture; that in fact, Joe Vigil had no legal right to the ditch registered at the state engineer's office in Santa Fe; that consequently, I owed him nothing; that Vigil habitually blocked the water at the head of the ditch when Shipton was using it, and blamed it on the beavers; that he, Shipton, had paid his dues on the other ditch and that Ernie Gurule, who was not a bad guy, would verify it; and furthermore, that Joe Vigil was not to be trusted any further than I could throw him.

Back in La Madera, the church bell announced Good Friday services. Someone had stolen my water.

Saturday morning, ditch-cleaning day, I left early to walk the half mile upstream to Gurule's farm. I found a likely place to ford the river, and stripping down to a shirt, tossed my clothes and boots across, and stepped in. The water was so cold that it burned. Rio Servilleta had grown up overnight into a throbbing torrent: dead branches swept past on their way to Rio Vallecitos, Rio Ojo Caliente, Rio Chama, Rio Grande, the Gulf of Mexico; river cobbles scraped along the bottom with the hollow sound of rock on rock. It was not the river I had seen first in October: the meager, tepid flow, clotted with algae, kept from drying up altogether by a few watercress seeps. I waded in to my knees, and braced myself with the shovel against a current that threatened to take my feet from under me. In midstream the water broke over my thighs; I could hold my own until I started to take a step, then the river would gain an edge. Poised there, it occurred to me that if I went under no one would even miss me.

I threw the shovel to the far bank and swam for it. Pulling myself out on some willows, I hustled back upstream, shivering, afraid that someone would drive by and see me running naked along the river bank at seven in the morning. I dressed and climbed out of the bottom past a big cottonwood where a raven was cleaning his feathers in the new sun.

Alfalfa was beginning to show in the field above, the leaves still folded in on one another. I crossed the field to what was left of my irrigation ditch, a furrow grown over with skeletons of tumbleweed. Vigil had already cleared the ditch on his side of the fence with a tractor blade. His cows were ambling down from the bed ground among the hillside junipers. I picked up a rock and threw it at a youngster who was nosing through my fence. Let him go, I thought after I had thrown it. Let him bloat up and die on that young alfalfa.

Instead of following the ditch, I climbed to the morada

through thornbushes — scourges for the penitent, I thought, remembering names from a field guide. Crucifixion bush. Crown of thorns.

A dead heifer lay by the doorway in back. She hadn't been dead long, the carcass was not even swollen. Dogs had been at her, starting from both ends. The door was boarded up, but I got in through a broken window. Someone had lived there. A table and chair stood in the middle room, maybe the kitchen; the rooms on the north and south were empty. The rats had moved in, building nests on top of the wall between rafters. But no wooden saints. No souls in torment.

An old government survey showed a road running past Gurule's to the old house, but only a trace of it remained. I walked along the ditch in the shade of the hill to the Gurule farm: a gray cement-plastered two-story adobe, a chicken yard where the hens and a single unlikely peacock were warming their skins in the sunshine, corrals, a railroad-tie barn, a log bridge spanning the river.

I waited for the others at the far end of the sheep pasture, drying myself on the rocks. Stopping once to look at the ewes, two men drove across the field in a pickup. I said hello to Ernie Gurule, the ditch boss, who with his Genghis Khan beard looked like he ought to be riding a black charger and swinging a battle axe; and to his older brother Pete, too frail, I thought, to be digging ditches. Pete chatted with me while we leaned on our shovels and watched Joe Vigil and two other men approach along the ditch.

"So you're the new owner," said Pete. "What are you doing way out here in the middle of nowhere?"

"Just trying to get along, I guess, same as you guys."

The two men were Vigil's sons; Walter, who was built like a

haystack, and who swung his shovel playfully at Ernie Gurule; and Frank, who shook my hand, but wouldn't look me in the eye. Joe didn't even nod in my direction.

The morning warmed quickly as we started to square the sides of the ditch and shovel loose sand from the bottom. Jackets and then shirts came off and were left hanging on branches along the way. I'd cleaned ditches before in Arroyo Hondo, but with forty men, working for nearly that many owners. In Hondo they would string out along the ditch and dig until the *majordomo* sang out, and the whole gang would move up at once, so that you worked in front of and behind the same two men all morning. But here they worked leapfrog. Each man moved when he felt like it, rested when he was tired, teamed up with anyone who needed help or conversation, worked until the work was done. Once the sweat began to run, I felt less alien. I felt as if these men were working for me and I for them, even though my work was only one-half of Gurule's and one third of Vigil's, and even though they could not have looked on me with anything other than curiosity, if not suspicion. I worked hard, but not any harder than my one man's worth.

We reached a place that was not a ditch at all, but a wide pool of red mud where cattails grew. I could see La Zorra from there — a few families, their fields and livestock, tucked into the end of the valley where Rio Servilleta emerged from a box canyon. (Narciso Martínez, the proprietor of the La Madera cantina, had spoken of it when I'd first come to town: "La Zorra. That means 'the fox.' Maybe it's a real fox. Maybe it's a lady. Who knows?")

On the other side of the pool the ditch ran below a gravelly cliff face. When it thawed, hunks of the cliff had sloughed off into the ditch. We had to dig a whole new ditch through the rubble.

[46]

"See what I mean, Arnold?" Vigil stood on the ditch bank and spoke down to me in the hole. "Two years ago the whole thing came down, and it took four days with the backhoe to fix it, *que no,* Ernie? It would have taken us all spring with the shovels, and by then the river would have been too low to go into the ditch. This river dries up in June, *que no,* Ernie?"

Gurule gave me a serious look and nodded his agreement.

"So if you want to use the water you have to pay us for our work, cause we don't work for nothing. You don't work for nothing, do you, Arnold? Shipton never gave us a penny, then when he wanted to irrigate we told him he had to pay first, and he got mad and called me bad names."

"He told me on the phone last night that he paid you."

"He's a liar," said Vigil. "He never paid, did he, Ernie?"

"No, never." Gurule started digging. Joe jumped into the ditch and worked beside him.

It was afternoon by the time Ernie Gurule opened the head-gate. We washed the mud from our shovels and headed back down. As we turned the bend by the cliff, I heard someone moaning. It was the old woman with the dogs. She was on the other side of the river, her arms clasped around a tree trunk, head thrown back, as if trying to convince someone to come down out of the treetops.

"Who's that?" I asked Walter.

"Pascualita Maestas. She's crazy. But don't worry, she can take care of herself. The dogs look after her."

In his Sunday best, Carlos Trujillo dropped by Easter morning with a couple of dark-eyed grandchildren to see who we were and what we were up to. Molly had driven over the night before and we were standing within the imaginary walls of our home, debating whether to build a fireplace or buy a stove. I'd seen Trujillo plowing with a new Ford tractor in the field immediately across the bridge, and I knew his name from the title abstract. His hair was turning white, but he had all of it, and he carried himself like a man of thirty. Like old man Montoya, he looked more Indian than not. I was getting the uncanny feeling that I'd met all these people somewhere before, like Dorothy in the Land of Oz, and that each of them had their counterpart in the life I had left behind on the other side of the Rio Grande.

"Nice place you've got here," said Carlos. "I used to own it, bought it for one hundred dollars, but that was a while back." The locals liked to see me wince when they told me how little La Junta had sold for in the past. "Used to hunt over here when I was a boy — pheasant, quail, turkey. Fish, too. Used to get big browns out of these beaver ponds, but that was when there was more water, and it was colder. Clear, too. The mining was what ruined the river. Not enough water for trout now — too dirty, and too warm. Suckers, that's about all."

"Any good to eat?"

"No, but we catch them anyway. They make good fertilizer for the garden, is all. What are you making here, Tom?" he asked, peeking into my trenches. "Concrete foundation? Put a lot of rocks in there before you pour, save on concrete that way. Where's your front door? Over there? No, don't put it over there, too icy in the wintertime, put it on the east or the south. What's it going to be? Frame?"

I told him we were planning to build it out of adobe, laying the bricks the long way through the wall, the way the old houses had been built.

"Why? That's too much work. You'll still be out here laying adobes in December. Yeah, I wanted to build a house over there, but my wife wanted to stay in town."

"Why's that?"

"Oh, I guess she was afraid of the drunks. You haven't had any trouble yet, have you?"

"No, not yet."

"They like to hang out over there across the road."

I felt as if I were just now getting around to reading the fine print.

"Yeah, Tom, you've got a nice place. I never should have sold it."

"Who bought it from you?"

"Benigno Vigil. You know him? He lives in that house on the corner."

"Any relation to Joe Vigil?"

"No, no relation. Benigno's the one that cleared the land and put in this little ditch so he could irrigate. I never did much of anything with the place."

"You've probably heard by now. I've got troubles with Joe Vigil over this ditch."

"What kind of troubles, Tom?"

"I thought I bought the place clear of debt from Hal Shipton, but Vigil says I owe him for maintaining the ditch the last five years. I don't know who to believe."

"That's my son-in-law, Harold Shipton. I used to irrigate for him over here when he owned the place. Yeah, him and Joe used to fight like cats and dogs over this ditch. I'd set the dams and then as soon as I was gone Joe would send one of his wetbacks over to put the water in his field, then I'd have to chase back over here and break Joe's dams, and it would go on like that all summer. I got pretty sick of the both of them . . . Say, Tom, how about renting me your pasture? My uncle's got some horses. He wanted me to ask you if you'd rent your place out."

"How many horses?"

"Two for now."

"Is your uncle's name Montoya?"

"Yeah, that's him."

"He was by a couple of days ago. I told him I didn't want to keep any horses, they tear the place up too bad. But let me think about it."

"Cows are worse. Course, if you don't want to rent, that's up to you. Bueno, Tom. Come over, meet the family."

Four riders crossed the bridge early next morning: Joe Vigil, Walter Vigil, and two wetbacks. The Vigils rode down towards the beaver swamp while the Mexicans swam their horses across the river and punched the cows out of the cedars, slapping their saddles to wake up the sleepy ones. With the cows in the field, the wetbacks loped to Gurule's fence and back, mouthing the fresh horses, scaring up strays out of the brush. They had the whole bawling lot of them across the river in ten minutes, while Joe and Walter pushed a few more out of the swamp. One of the wetbacks took the road and headed the herd towards Petaca as they funneled through the gate. The cows had just cleared the way when a third wetback drove Joe's pickup through the open gate, followed a few minutes later by the other brother, Frank Vigil, on the tractor. While the riders drove the cows up the road to summer pasture in the mountains, Frank bladed the Benigno Vigil ditch from my fence on up, and the Mexicans came behind, setting dams every twenty yards or so with rocks and sod. They had the water in the fields by the time I got to work on my trenches. I waved at Frank as he drove out, but he pretended not to see me.

It rained all that week. Vigil's pasture flooded and overflowed into our pasture where the trailer was parked, a ship at sea. We sat inside and played cards, wiping the steam from the window between hands to see if the rain had stopped.

One morning I was baling the water from the trenches to keep frost out of the footings when our pup bristled at something across the road. He took off barking, the bottom dropping out of his voice from the hound in him, and flushed an elderly gentleman out of the trees at the top of the ridge. It was the droopy-eyed one who took his constitutional from La Madera to La Zorra each morning. He held a bough in one hand, like some local woodland deity, and spoke softly to the dog as he picked his way down the ridge. "Go home. Get along, now." He marched across the road and through the gate as if he had an appointment to see me.

"Benigno Vigil is the name."

I told him mine.

"There will be piñon nuts in the fall," he announced, showing me the branch. "In years past they harvested these forests by the carload. You can expect a bumper crop once every seven years. Do you like piñon nuts?"

I told him I did.

"You must be the young man who purchased the property

from Mr. Shipton. I purchased it from Mr. Trujillo for three hundred dollars when it was still a wilderness, many years ago. I grew up in La Madera, but I worked in California for thirty-five years before I returned. They offered me the postmaster's job here in town, you see."

"I understand that you're the one who made this ditch."

"That's right. I dug it all by hand with Mr. Jaramillo, who helped, though he was never much for physical labor. He owned the adjacent property, now owned by Mr. Vigil. Of course, I had to hire a man with a bulldozer to clear and level the land before I planted the alfalfa. Before that nothing grew here but willows and cottonwood trees. Yes, Mr. Jaramillo and I dug this ditch with shovels."

"Did you ever fight over the water?"

"Oh no. You see, Mr. Jaramillo allowed me to put the ditch through his property with the understanding that I would maintain it and that he could use the water when he wished, though he was not much of a farmer and seldom did. He was the schoolmaster, you understand, and not very interested in agricultural matters. We never had any disagreement. Of course, when Mr. Shipton bought the property from me, he and Mr. Vigil fought all the time. Once they nearly came to blows right there in Mr. Vigil's store. May I ask, are you having difficulty with Mr. Vigil over the use of the ditch?"

"Yes, I am. He says I owe him money because Shipton was delinquent on the maintenance of the ditch."

"Well, if you'll take some neighborly advice, I think you'll find Mr. Vigil to be a fairly reasonable man, very much respected around here; but I would be careful with his son Frank, he's a little touchy. He's a lawyer in Santa Fe now, and I think success has gone to his head. He thinks he's a cut above the rest of us now. They have lots of property, the Vigils. Well-to-do people. They call this Frank's place. He'll inherit it, you understand, when his father dies."

"Is Mr. Jaramillo still living?"

"Oh yes, he lives right there next to Mr. Martínez's bar. You see, the river changed its course when he owned Mr. Vigil's land, and not being much for work, he neglected to sandbag the bank until it was too late and the river washed out the old road, which ran right through here where you're building your house . . . but I can see, I'm keeping you from your work, aren't I? I like to walk along here, so you'll see from time to time. I'm not young any more, and I must keep active."

He marched off towards his house on the corner: the row of umbrella trees in front pruned to within an inch of their lives, the woodpile in back a marvel of geometric precision. I wondered what would become of La Madera after all its old men died.

Frank Vigil was leaning on the counter reading a newspaper when I came to ask for the water a few days later. He looked to see who it was and kept reading. He took after his mother, round-faced and pretty, instead of his father, whose looks were on the bulldoggish side. We were about the same age, which if anything widened the differences between us. We had never yet spoken, and if my land and the land that was to be his didn't meet at a barbed wire fence, we probably never would have had two words for each other.

Frank's mother was sitting behind the counter. She told me

[53]

that Joe had gone to the mountains, and that he would be in the store after five to do the books. I would have left then but for the feigned deafness of the man behind the newspaper. I would make him look at me, at least, this time. If not for the sake of the water, then for its own sake.

"Frank."

He folded the newspaper slowly and dropped it on the counter.

"I'm going to be using the water if you're done with it."

"Are you asking me or telling me?" He was looking at the toes of my boots.

"You've had the water in your field for more than a week."

"Pay first, then you can have it."

"I don't owe you anything. There's a survey at the state engineer's office in Santa Fe that says I have a right to use that water. It also says that you don't have any legal right to the use of the ditch, but I'm willing to forget about that. I'm not interested in keeping you from using the water. I just want to use it myself."

"Sue me then," he said. "See how far your survey gets you. Your property was abandoned for twenty years. You forfeited your ditch rights. All I have to do is pick up that phone right there and the state engineer will tear your survey up. Happens to be my cousin."

He stood up, stretched, and scratched his belly.

"I'd better talk to the boss," I said, probing for the nerve, some sign of life. "Tell your dad I'll be over to see him tonight."

La Madera's two mercury vapor lamps were burning when we parked in front of Vigil's store at dusk. Joe was behind the counter, writing in a ledger.

"Hello, Arnold, what can I do for you?" Friendly. As if we'd come in for a loaf of bread.

"My wife had a few questions she wanted to ask you, if you can spare the time."

That got his attention. In La Madera a man never spoke to a woman on business, but Vigil seemed to enjoy the novelty of it.

"Yes?" he said to Molly.

"Mr. Vigil, it's about our problem with the water."

"Problem? What problem? There's no problem as long as you pay me the fifty dollars."

I didn't want to listen. I went out into the warm evening and sat down next to the gasoline pump. The toads were at it in Sanchez's bog. It was so soft and peaceful out there that it hardly mattered to me what was being said inside. I felt like a boy again, without any of the cares of ownership. For a minute I was sitting again on the shore of a lake in Connecticut, listening to the frogs croaking in the lily pond. Molly and Joe stood behind the glass picture window, on a stage of blue light. Molly jawed wordlessly at him. Joe looked humble, for once.

It was fully dark when they came out.

"Let's go, Arnold, we're going to see Mr. Jaramillo and settle this thing once and for all."

The three of us paraded across the plaza to a tidy house between the Sanchez place and Narciso's bar. A man in clothes too big for him answered the door, his face the color and texture of a cured tobacco leaf. Mr. Jaramillo ushered us into the living room and offered Molly a chair. He turned off the television. It was dark until Joe screwed a light bulb into a table lamp.

"I was the first one to have a television in La Madera," said Mr. Jaramillo, making the best of an uncomfortable situation.

[55]

"Mr. Jaramillo . . ." Joe, stealing the role of plaintiff, addressed the bench. "Mr. and Mrs. Arnold owe me fifty dollars for work I did on the Benigno Vigil ditch, but they don't want to pay. Will you tell them please how their property was abandoned for so many years?"

"Ireland," I said. "My name is Ireland, like the country."

"Let me see, let me see," said Mr. Jaramillo, rubbing his cheek and consulting the ceiling. "Ah yes, I remember now. Mr. Arnold, your property was abandoned for many many years. Mr. Vigil here is one of our little town's best citizens. He helps people all the time. He wouldn't try to cheat you. Be a good boy and pay him the fifty dollars."

Molly looked at me as if to say "I've had it. It's up to you now." Somewhere along the way I had lost the point.

"You'll have your money tomorrow, Joe."

Everybody shook hands. Mr. Jaramillo showed us to the door.

"Nice to meet you, Mr. Arnold," he said. "You're new around here, aren't you?"

When I got up the next morning, a full head of water was running in the ditch and spilling into the field below the house site. Joe Vigil had brought his tractor and opened up the dam at the other end, so we would have plenty. Already, the alfalfa was looking greener than it had any right to be.

DOG DAYS

The dogs are awake tonight. I hear them up and down the valley, rejoicing in their evil secret.

At my back door, I face the thief of love: a loveworn stray from town, part chow or malamute, who knows as all his cousins know that my Chloe is in heat, the almost-virgin Chloe, locked in the cab of the pickup. The ruffian has a black ring around one eye and in the bleary light of the breezeway he is the color of ashes. He regards me without fear, as if I were nothing more than an inconvenience, a fence to go around but not through.

All night long they will come like pilgrims to a shrine, pausing to consider the sheep and read dogsign on the fenceposts, then nosing the tires of the pickup in search of Chloe — poor, lovesick, twice-had Chloe, named after a dead goldfish.

When I was a boy in New York City, my parents wouldn't let us have a dog.

"It's cruel to keep a dog in an apartment," my father said. "No place for him to run, and a dog will go crazy all cooped up in an apartment house."

My father had grown up on a farm, so he knew all about dogs.

"But old Mr. Hespel has that little Chihuahua," argued my sister, who really wanted a horse.

"Goes to show," said my father. "That dog's as crazy as Hespel, and almost as mean."

But I wanted a dog anyway. I swore that someday I'd have a place where a dog could run all day if he pleased.

Danny Dillon lived on our street in a red brick townhouse. His father, a big florid cop from the 37th Precinct, had a spiteful retriever called Blackie. One day we were playing in Danny's back yard, a concrete oven with barbed wire strung at one end to keep the burglars out of the alleys. When I grabbed Danny around the neck in fun, Blackie went for me. I remember the rubbery pink corners of his mouth, the warmth of the jaws, and Danny standing there saying "Bad dog!" as if Blackie were chewing on a living-room rug. Blackie was not to blame, Mr. Dillon said later, he was only trying to protect Danny. My shirt was torn but the skin was unbroken, only a faint dappled blush below the rib cage, as if a lip-sticked aunt had kissed me there.

My childhood moved thereafter through a maze of waiting teeth. I began to cross the street to avoid a dog on a leash, and I would detour clear around the block to escape one running loose. "A dog can smell your fear," my father told me, so if it were not bad enough to be afraid, I wore an aura of fear that would attract dogs and make my friends hold their noses the way they did around Stinky Charlie in my second-grade class.

I gave up wanting a dog until I made friends with Bob, a beagle in the heyday of beagles, who lived with my Aunt Iris and Uncle Harvey on their farm in Delaware. When Aunt Iris had me deliver a bowl of milk to the colony of cats in the barn, Bob followed. He followed me through the oily, hoof-cratered bog in the horse pasture to the dead tree where a tire hung from a rope. When I crossed the yard to wheedle a biscuit from my grandmother, Bob would pat along behind as if I were someone important and he, being only a dog, did not really deserve my company. He'd wait by my grandmother's screen door for me, looking awfully hurt until I came back out and said "C'mon Bob." He would have followed me anyway, finding my dreamy pokings closer to his own pace than Uncle Harvey's farm work. We made a covenant, Bob and I. He was to be my dog, and I his boy, and no one else was to know. Then one winter we got a letter from Aunt Iris saying that Bob had been hit by a truck.

I never really had a dog of my own until we moved to La Junta. Molly and I agreed that it had to be a hound, because we were mule people, and where there were mules, there were hounds. We found Jake in the limestone hill country of west Texas under the crabby auspices of his mother, a full-blooded redbone bitch from Arkansas with teats like parsnips. Jake Fletcher, the itinerant preacher who owned her, didn't know who the father was, but half a hound was better than no hound at all.

"Keep an eye on that bitch, she's liable to skin you alive when she's got pups," said the preacher as Molly crawled under the porch and dragged out the red one with the sorry face.

It was Jake. "Name a good dog after a bad man," they say, so we named him after all the damning rumors we'd heard about Father Fletcher.

Jake has almost lived up to his name. Not a bad dog, but good for nothing; ugly to strangers, but not the slathering man-eater I wish for when cars park across the road; aware of livestock, but more likely to bat his eyelashes at trespassing cows than to run them off; ignorant of skunks and porcupines, but no threat to gophers either; homeloving, though a neighbor once spotted him near a freshly killed ewe.

The best I can say for Jake is that he survives. Once he got shot. The bullet passed clear through his rear end without touching bone or vital organ. Then he got run over. It peeled the last six inches of his tail clean to the bone, and we amputated. To Jake the shame of that stump was worse than the injury. For days he tried to walk away from it, and failing in that, would measure it tenderly with his tongue to see if it were growing back. If not a good dog, we have an educated one, and much too homely for anyone to steal.

Now the Australian shepherd Chloe has come to us — Chloe and her suitors, who appear in the moonlit yard night after night like the creatures of a fevered dream. Her sister, Smoky, a blue wraith who promised to be our working dog, vanished in a thunderstorm. Chloe, the orphan of the litter, made up the loss. She came in February, in that inert moment of the year when what has been and what is about to be blink at one another across a vacant space of days. In that empty time, she was something. On the morning of her arrival, the goldfish Chloe died of winter, belly-up in the algae.

Ours was to be a tidy two-dog farm, immune from the town and its plague of mongrels. Chloe will have her pups anyway. They will look like Jake, or the other one. They will infest the doorway. They will dig holes where I do not want holes. They will get underfoot and whimper to come inside where it's warm. And when the time comes to get rid of them, there's sure to be at least one we can't bear to give away.

The Ravens of La Junta

The choice of place had been the first and last choice, overriding all considerations of what we were going to do after the house was built and the money ran out. At the time, it was enough just to be there and watch the winter coming on. We believed that if you could only put yourself *where* you wanted to be, the *what* would take care of itself — a faith that wore thin over the years, but at the time, one that possessed our whole hearts.

The place had to be far from the cities, where both of us had grown up and been educated, so we could renounce the values we thought cities and education represented and start again from scratch. It had to have water for irrigation, so we could grow things. It had to be beautiful; not obviously beautiful, but beautiful in a way that would keep its beauties secret from others and reveal them, through many seasons and careful watching, to us. And for me, so I could pursue my fantasy of being a field naturalist, it had to have wild places to walk in and wild creatures of one kind or another to look at and write about. Thinking of it now, ten years later, it seems that it had to be that place and none other — those neglected fields at the junction of the two rivers that still managed to look alive when the alfalfa came up, that piece of gray earth by the road waiting to receive its new antique house.

The house was nowhere near finished when we moved in that November, the first to be spent in La Madera. Molly was two months pregnant. We had a bed, a table and two chairs, and a wood-burning cookstove that was to be the hub of our existence through the cold months ahead. Its firebox was a size meant for cooking, not heating, but it beat freezing our tails in the Kozy Koach, where the only heat had been from a trailer-sized gas oven. Between the first frost and the decision to move into the unfinished house, we had wrapped ourselves in blankets every morning, turned on the oven full blast, and stood as close to it as we could get, drinking coffee until our breath ran down the windows.

The idea of the house, if not its design, had been conceived in a motel room in Farmington, New Mexico, more than two years before building it. Lost and frightened, and not knowing exactly where we were going next, we sat on the motel bed and cried the tears of the homeless. It was time to settle down and make a nest, we decided. It didn't matter where it was or what it looked like, as long as it was ours.

Born of an image of New England coziness (hints of a Nantucket saltbox, and one of its models had been a limestone cottage in Fredericksburg, Texas), the house looked old even when it was new. It had wooden windows on three sides, a stovepipe coming crookedly through the roof at the ridge, and the look of a house that was warm and comfortable inside — the kind of house that lost and frightened children come upon in fairy tales just as they are about to give up hope. For washing, it had a cast-iron sink on sawhorses with a bucket for a drain. I'd had the foresight to dig a hole in the yard for a toilet and build a windy little shelter around it for privacy; in an inventory of buildings and furnishings, early Spanish missionaries referred to their outhouse as *lugar de la necesidad secreta,* the place of secret necessity. We pumped water from the well with a borrowed handpump, chopped wood, ate a lot of pancakes, and were mostly happy, with the happiness that comes from being in difficult circumstances and making do.

The day after Thanksgiving it snowed eighteen inches, and the morning after that, the thermometer read twenty below. I toasted my shins by the cookstove, drank tea, and looked out the window. We had already been there through three seasons and done a lot of looking at the mountain and the river junction, but this was something entirely different.

The snow gave me a chance to write in my journal for the first time since the previous April, when the housebuilding had started: "When I imagine what I would really like to do during my lifetime, I keep coming back to the study of an animal or a community of animals in their natural habitat."

Ethology had taken a long time coming into its own as a science. Among others, the young Charles Darwin had longed to break the confines of laboratory and museum, see faraway places, and come to grips with the dragons of speculative science. He went on board the *Beagle* assuming only that the world and its creatures were not what they were assumed to be, and that only by seeing them for ourselves could we discover their true nature. Lying seasick in his berth for weeks on end, he must have had to confront his own romantic notions of what the life of a field naturalist was about.

About the closest I'd ever come to studying animals was Primate Behavior. The professor was a baboon specialist. We, his students, watched endless films of baboons picking lice out of one another's hair and cracking them between their teeth like pistachios; baboons roosting in trees in the African dusk; adolescent baboons coming testily into their own at the edge of baboon society. I saw the rear ends of receptive female baboons turn pomegranate red. I witnessed the brief and absent-minded matings of baboons (the male always seemed to be engrossed in something in the far distance); their theater of threat and submission; baboons moving by the hundreds through the liquid heat of the Kalahari; and baboons just hanging out with the flies. But what intrigued me far more than the baboons was the invisible presence of the researcher (in this case, my professor), who got to live under those immense skies for months at a stretch, cook over a fire, sleep in a tent, and indulge in long, meditative silences, all the more silent for the ceaseless voices of insects, birds, and carrion mongers; and who, besides taking a few notes now and then, had nothing to do but watch and listen.

I'd never seriously entertained the idea of living such a life, but it was nice to think about it, with the kind of fondness people have for distant, inaccessible things (mountain peaks, old loves). And in small, vicarious ways, maybe it could still be experienced. "If I am to be an ethologist," I wrote that November, "I must be one wherever I happen to be, if not in the rain forest with the prosimians, then by my fireside, with the spiders."

In December, a red-tailed hawk began to appear in the sky over La Junta, sometimes sailing directly overhead, cocking its head, checking out the new inhabitants. Red tails had been important to me ever since I'd moved to the Southwest, appearing time and again when I most needed guidance, or at least, the conviction of being watched over. The appearance of a red tail always meant something, even if it was impossible to say exactly what. More often than not, I would decide it meant "Do what your heart tells you to do," neatly avoiding right and wrong.

This particular hawk appeared twice without offering any guidance, only "Who are you and what are you doing here?" The third time, he was circling in a way that showed he wasn't very hungry, just cruising, when a lone raven came up from behind and began taking short, menacing passes at him. The hawk took his sweet time moving on, but troubled himself every now and then to flap his wings and stay out of harm's way. Slowly, the raven drove the interloper west until they both disappeared into a canyon on the other side of town.

I chewed on that one for weeks. Maybe the hawk represented the freedom of youth. Maybe that freedom was being displaced by domestic responsibility — the raven. Ravens were a species I had overlooked until then, setting my sights on the scarce, godlike raptors, the eagles and hawks. With a baby on the way, maybe it was time to come down to earth.

That winter all of our living was done in the one room downstairs — the living room. Before moving in we had poured a mud floor, finished with linseed oil instead of the traditional lamb's blood because we had been told that blood floors attracted flies. We didn't get our first lamb, an orphan, until the spring. Ethyl, the goat, lived in a makeshift wire pen on the other side of the outhouse. Her bag, which nearly dragged on the ground, always inspired wonder. Jake, the dog, carved out a cave for himself in the haystack. The first coat of mud plaster went on the inside walls of the house to keep the wind from blowing through the spaces between the adobes, but somehow or other it kept finding its way in, and with it, windborn sprays of snow. The fire was allowed to die out at bedtime. One morning, I woke to find that a glass of water left on the table overnight had iced over.

You could hardly walk out the door without seeing ravens in the newly bare branches of the cottonwoods along the river or swarming over the neighbor's cow pasture. I had no binoculars then, but ravens were big enough to be seen without them. They didn't fly off to the tropics with the other birds. You could sit in your warm house on a cold morning, eat pancakes, and watch ravens, all at the same time. They weren't timid. A raven would gladly sun itself on a fencepost by the road, provided the cars kept moving and the people stayed inside. They may not have been especially exotic, or colorful, or musical, but they had their qualities, not the least of which was their knack of living off civilization, while so many others were being overrun by it. And while it was hard to accept that anything so common could be a worthy object of study, here was a ready and abundant source of meaning, something that could rescue me from common tasks and common perceptions at almost any moment without ever leaving home.

"Large numbers of vocal, restive ravens flying low means snowstorm," I wrote, never satisfied with events until they had been stamped with their significance. There was precedence for this sort of observation. The ancient Greeks and Romans read the future in the flight of birds. They also read the configuration of their entrails, much as the ancient Chinese could read the hexagons of a turtle's shell, although it always mystified me how anyone could tell one set of entrails from another. Our local birds were mainly concerned with local varieties of war, plague, and famine. Three ducks flying upstream: buy groceries.

I also appreciated ravens for their blackness, learning a new verb in this connection: iride. Black feathers could iride green or

blue or rainbow colors, like an oil spill on pavement after a rain, depending on the angles of light and attention. Black was the union of all colors, we had been taught in high school, not the absence of it, and compared to a raven against new snow, almost everything else in life seemed mediocre. And their thrift. They were frequently judged for liking carrion (the rottener it was, the better they seemed to like it), it being politer to kill animals for food than to find them already dead. And their playfulness. Ravens seemed to be getting more fun out of life than they deserved. In flight, one would often tuck its wings, go into a head-long dive, and spin halfway or, if eyes did not deceive, even completely around before turning itself right, just for kicks.

But what most attracted me to ravens was their talent for being themselves. You could tell by looking at them that they did not particularly care to be anything else. They did not worry about the burdensome responsibilities of home and parenthood, or the list of things that those responsibilities might keep them from doing. They had no use for manners, at least not in the sense of behaving the way others thought it was appropriate for them to behave. All their manners, here in the sense of what they did — the way that one was stropping its beak on the branch, for example, with no thought of something else it would rather or better be doing — came from the inside out. There was no pretense in them, and no apology.

We stayed close to home and did what we could to make it more comfortable. A foam pad covered the stairwell (there were no stairs yet, only a ladder) and kept our precious little heat from escaping. We were fiercely practical. At one point we had seriously considered building the living room over the animal pens, the way we had heard that certain Scandinavian farmers did, so that the heat from manure would rise into the house. What was known as "upstairs," without a floor, and with nothing between it and the great outdoors but a thin skin of corrugated steel nailed to one-by-fours, was used mainly as an observatory. From the window on the west, I could keep an eye on what was happening across the road, where dangerous men parked and drank at all hours of the day and night. In January, they hooked my front gate onto their rear bumper and drove away (an old gag), dragging down about thirty yards of barbed-wire fence. The French doors on the east, supposed to lead to a balcony at some time in the future, looked out on Rio Servilleta, a beaver pond, the hayfields and hills. Beavers were quickly cutting down the few remaining narrowleaf cottonwoods along that stretch, but nothing could be done about it, no more than the neighbor's deranged cow could be kept on the neighbor's side of the fence. She raided our haystack a few times, and once, rubbing against the house in the night, cracked a window pane.

That was the month I learned that most of the birds I had been calling ravens were crows. Being from the East, I had been letting myself believe that the one was just a western race of the other, but no. As one of Sholom Aleichem's characters says, if you are trying to tell the sex of a goat, you must look for "certain unmistakable signs." Ravens were bigger than crows, for one thing, but "bigger" wasn't much help unless you had one of each in front of you at the same time for comparison. Not so easy. The two species did not generally associate. Ravens had a roman nose, said the book, and when they perched, their throat feathers had a characteristic shagginess, or "goiter." Ravens, unlike crows, walked on the ground, but seldom hopped. Seen in flight from below, ravens had a pointed, spade-shaped tail, whereas a crow's tail was rounded like a fan. And the voices of the two were different: ravens croaked, crows cawed.

Right from the start, this eliminated most of the large, black birds that were in the habit of congregating near the house. In the field guide, the shaded area representing the geographical range of ravens covered a large part of the western hemisphere from Alaska to Tierra del Fuego, including my part of it. The ideal thing would be to find a mated pair and follow them day by day through their lives, faithfully recording their dramas of homemaking and reproduction, the rearing of young ravens, their competition for food, the pair's unfailing devotion to one another and to the defense of the home territory — in fact, the very dramas I found myself in the midst of, but which were too close to home to be very interesting compared to the dramas of wild ravens. The journal of that winter is full of solitary walks and rapturous sightings of birds (water ouzel, pigeon hawk, great horned owl, and for the first time in March, the sandhill cranes), but almost nothing on the natural wonder that was taking place inside the steeply pitched house at the side of the road, our place of secret necessity, where money and firewood were being so carefully rationed, and where a small human life was preparing to greet mine. Nature was something to be observed out of doors, in the form of ravens, for example. At home, in the form of an unborn child, it was almost too awesome for words.

The inevitability of that event, also its finality, the thought that once it had taken place there would be no going back, took me up along the ridges and down into the arroyos and bosques. The wild world was getting away from me more quickly than I had planned. Domesticity was catching up.

It was hard enough to find one raven, harder yet to find a pair, and hardest to find what I wanted most, a pair that could be identified as the same pair I had seen the last time — *those* ravens, as opposed to just any ravens. I bought a notebook to write down all the things I was going to learn about ravens when I found some. It was called *The Ravens of La Junta.* If the ravens never turned up at La Junta, the title could always be changed, depending on where they did. "Raven on fencepost," I wrote on page one. Or on page two, getting more into the spirit of things, "Lone raven in the dead cottonwood south of Uvaldo's, about 8 a.m." They had this annoying habit, once they knew they were being observed, of flying away.

There had to be a place where ravens could be depended on to come with regularity. The book said that ravens spent a good part of each day foraging by themselves, but they roosted together in numbers at night. The trick was to find the roost, or better yet, if spring ever came, a nest — "a large mass of sticks, bones, wool on a cliff." We happened to have some cliffs not too far from the house in a place known as La Cueva. I passed it every time I drove to town: about sixty acres of bottomland, a wide bend in the river, and beyond it, the yellow, honeycombed cliffs, in the absence of any real wilderness, standing for wildness, danger, and inaccessibility. It wouldn't have taken more than ten minutes to park the truck and walk across the pasture, but then it would no longer have been the place I wanted it to be. A secret place needed a secret entrance.

Meanwhile, a lot still had to be done at home before the baby arrived. I'd salvaged part of the basketball court from the old high school gymnasium in Ojo Caliente and was slowly piecing it back together upstairs as our bedroom floor. Like everything else in that house, this floor had the look of antiquity from the very start. You could see pieces of the out-of-bounds line on it, and it had been preworn by generations of hormone-crazed teenagers. Downstairs, the holes that the wind whistled through were chinked with sheep's wool. "A house *needs* a few holes in it so you can breathe," I declared, chinking. Molly plastered the adobe walls with a mixture of sand from a roadcut north of town and our own dear, gray dirt. She said this would "keep the dirt down." Molly's mother, Mary Alice, insisted that a house with a baby in it also have running water, so the plumbing, at least enough for a kitchen sink and a bathtub, was going to get installed with the help of uncles Pat and George. Principles weaken over the years. We lived to regret our conscientious objections to hot-water heaters and toilets.

"So many weeks pass between long walks," I wrote, "that I'm beginning to wonder if the ravens live mainly in my imagination, or if that's not as it should be anyway."

It was February, and the snow was beginning to melt, before I got to La Cueva. From our house, the way led across our river, the Servilleta (ours because it bisected the property, and distinct from theirs, the Vallecitos, which merely bordered it), up the arroyo where the chokecherries grew, through the fence, and up over the initial rise of the mountain, a hump between the two drainages. Someone had dug a couple of pits at the top of the hump, probably exploratory mines, but in the mythology of this walk, open graves waiting to accept the bones of dead naturalists. Only there did I leave the sight and therefore the influence of home and plunge into thickets of scrub oak, mountain mahogany, and privet, the fastnesses of rabbits. Then down through a patch of sumac

[73]

meadow to the Vallecitos, following cow paths when the purposes of the cows coincided with mine, or squeezing through the brush when they didn't. The riverbank narrowed and disappeared more than once. Up and around through the rocks: saltbush, cholla. The year's first, faint warmth.

By the river again, I scared off a family of baby ducks. A pile of coyote scat, with its purple husks of juniper berries, had been immaculately deposited on a river rock. It meant I was on the trail: maybe not the *right* trail, but one trail or another; and the sense that goes along with trails, however deceptive, that they are leading somewhere. Once again I knew that old thrill, when first alone in a wild place, that makes you believe there are more and even greater thrills waiting up ahead.

The trace of a wagon road led to the shelf of treeless ground above the cliffs. Hard to believe in a country of barely seeping watercress seeps, a mineral spring gushed out of the side of the mountain. On slightly higher ground, a homesteader had built a hut of railroad ties and the crumbly yellow rock of the cliffs, big enough for one person only, and tight at that. If nothing else, the place was private. The wind blew constantly. It blew through the holes in the cliff and made a beastly moan. The gyppy water, not hot, not cold, formed mossy pools below, the home of many small, shrimplike critters, as strange to me as the Galapagos tortoises must have been to young Darwin. For its spring alone, the place was unlike any I had seen, so much water leaping from barren rock, such a miraculous height above the riverbottom, and in quantities that in this country, where water was always the exception, usually passed for a "river."

The homesteader had come to stay. Besides the shelter, he had dug irrigation ditches and terraced off a large garden, building up the borders with rock. He must have been more than a little eccentric to live off and away like that, trying to grow things with water that even corn would have a hard time loving. Maybe he had a taste for the watercress that grew along the margins of the moving water, like Suibhne (Sweeney) Geilt, an Irish madman of legend who craved that bitter, succulent vegetable and flew around the countryside competing with the other madmen for possession of the best watercress springs. Or maybe this homesteader had come to La Cueva for many of the same reasons that I had come to La Junta: because he liked being there by the gushing spring at the foot of the mountain with the wind and the porcupines and his salt-sick corn plants, drinking coffee in the morning while the sun took forever getting over the mountain, and so used to being alone that he didn't think of it any more than a fish thinks of the water. Maybe for him, too, the choice of place had been first and foremost.

It was a perfect place for ethology — far enough out of the way of human traffic to imagine I was much farther, water for attracting wildlife, long views, afternoon sun, even the makings of overnight shelter, with a little repair work. With a lot of patient sitting and watching, the other inhabitants, and the ravens especially, would come to accept me as part of the natural way of things. In the original sense of the word, I would be the genius of the place: its Panic spirit. Even though I would have to come and go, having to attend to family and property and all the other things that would certainly take me away, I would always return to sit and watch my beloved birds. It would be my place alone, removed from the world's storm and stress, the fixing of leaks, the crying of babies.

I walked along the edge of the cliffs, peeking into holes and crevices. There was always the chance that something would be looking back, and with that possibility, both hope and dread. It was the kind of place that mountain lions liked, and if I did not exactly want to meet one, I also did not exactly want to rule out the chance of meeting one, either.

Cholla, barrel cactus, and one I had never bothered to identify, but knew in my one-man taxonomy as crucifixion bush, grew at the base of the cliffs, maybe sixty feet below; but nothing much up above, where the wind was tearing at a few stubborn grasses. In one hole I found a shiny, hard, liver-colored mass, the accumulated scat of something considerably smaller than a lion, but alive, and living there. I stood at the edge and let the wind pummel me for a minute, scanning the riverbottom as if I already had some proprietory interest in cliffs and wind, something to protect against intruders. It wasn't enough just to have found such a place and to be exploring it, more or less free of responsibilities for the afternoon. I wanted to keep everybody else away.

I was still standing there when the raven blew up over the cliff and almost into my face. It must have scared him almost as much as it scared me, to be riding the blast sixty feet off the ground and then all of a sudden to be facing a man. He shat, climbed up out of the reach of harm, and held there at the closest safe distance to look again, reassembling his world into the kind of order he trusted it to have. (Ravens up. Men down.) Then he spoke. It was a sort of rattle, as much from the bowel as from the throat, and in it there was both fear and outrage: "This cliff is taken. You are not wanted here." He drifted north, riding the thermal, checking to see if there were any more of me around, then fell up and away into the bottomless sky.

Spring came at last, had to come. We were running out of firewood. The beavers finished cutting down the trees along the riverfront except for one, which for some reason known only to beavers, they gnawed halfway through and then left standing. The plumbing was in. We had a kitchen cabinet ("pie safe") from Texas with a zinc sheetmetal top and a flour drawer, the kind of thing that used to appear in mail-order catalogs long ago. And a home-made sink cabinet, painted an exquisite blue, about the only thing in the house not the color of earth. Hannah was born in June. I was watching a television show about chimpanzees when Molly had her first hard contraction. Having to drive to the hospital, I never got to see the end of the show.

I had already entered the wilderness and come face to face with a wild raven, so there didn't seem to be much point in going back to La Cueva. That year and all the years following, the ravens would build their nests, lay their eggs, and raise their young in private, as they would long after the house at La Junta, built to last forever, had melted back into the ground. I still took walks along the river, and once even went as far as sharpening up a machete and cutting a trail in the direction of La Cueva, but it never got very far. Hadn't I already created enough of a disturbance without putting in a road?

The following winter, to my disappointment, I discovered that the definitive work on wild ravens had already been written. It was all there, and in exhaustive detail — the raven's fidelity to its home territory and its mate, elaborate sexual displays, and yes, even their true-life dramas: "When one of a pair is lost the other will utter particular calls that were used by the lost partner but not by itself." The author also pointed out that one was most likely to find ravens, not on remote cliffs, but at "garbage tips, open-air slaughtering yards, battlefields, and other sources of abundant food." And sure enough, there they were at the La Madera dump every time I went to drop off the trash, joyously feasting on our deceased pets.

OUT OF WORK

I was working at the block plant out behind Conley's lumber mill in Arroyo Seco. Dry Gulch. One man ran a little bobcat loader tethered to a diesel generator with an extension cord that reeled in and out behind the operator's seat. He would scoop a bucketful of crushed pumice from the pile and dump it into the pug mill, an oversized cement mixer. Then he'd hop up on the platform over those murderous, churning egg beaters, break a bag of cement into the mixer, and hose down the mix. Too dry and the block would crumble when it came out of the press. Too wet and it would stick in the chute. It was my job to catch the fresh block on a plate, set it gingerly on a rack, and get back in time to catch the next one before the machine dumped it on the ground. On a day without breakdowns — a rare and hateful day — we could make a thousand blocks.

The wind blew so hard that the mix would jump the conveyor on its way from the pug mill to the press and pelt me like a summer hailstorm. As much as possible I worked with my eyes shut. By the end of the day I hurt all over and my pockets were full of pumice. I was sick of it. It was a great day when the high price of cement put me out of work.

We lived across the river from La Madera, right in the middle of things. Thirty-five miles to town no matter which way you traveled. Thirty-five miles to Española by way of Chamita, a town that never ran out of dogs no matter how many of them got run over; then across the Rio Grande on a shaky one-lane bridge. Thirty-five miles to Taos, if you took the washboard shortcut through the gorge, or twice that distance if you stayed on the highway. Thirty-five miles to Tres Piedras or Abiquiu, both like La Madera, almost too small to pass for towns.

When I got laid off at the block plant, my sheep were penned up and the hay was nearly gone. Before I could pasture them I had to build a fence to keep them out of the orchard, so I went to see my neighbor Dennis McKeever, a retired railroad man with a crest of white hair like a cottontop quail. We chatted for a while before I got around to asking him if I could borrow his digging bar so I could dig some postholes.

Previously, I had borrowed this particular bar from Dennis to dig the foundation for my house, so I was already on intimate terms with it. Even though it was bent up with jobs too big for it and as blunt as a baseball bat on the digging end, it worked, and I liked the heft of it. When I finished the foundation I tried to buy it from him, but he wouldn't hear of it. Instead, he told me to hold on to it, and if he needed it, he would borrow it from me.

Months passed, and Dennis never came for his bar. The newest addition to the family, it lived standing up in the outhouse with the other dirt tools, shovels and rakes, mattock and sledge. After you've used a certain tool for a while, it's natural to start feeling possessive towards it, and that's what happened with me and Dennis's bar. Being familiar, it made things go easier than another bar would have, even a straight, sharp, new one. But just as I had started to assume it was mine for keeps, sure enough, Dennis came and borrowed it back for some lost cause or other. That was the last I'd seen of it.

He rummaged around in the backyard and found a different,

heavier digging bar.

"I'd let you have this one," he said, "if I thought you were man enough to use it."

Finally he stumbled over my bar lying rusted in some weeds.

"Take it along," he said. "I've been meaning to take it in and get it fixed one of these days, but I'll tell you what. If I don't get around to it after a while, I'll sell it to you."

I went home and laid out my fence: posts every ten feet from the river crossing, past the two big cottonwoods, up along a bank, across the ditch, past the rhubarb, the quince, the black locust, the wild roses, the clothesline. I'd been taught that when a job has a hard part and a not-so-hard part, you're supposed to do the hard part first. So I started down by the river, where I'd have to sink the postholes in rocky ground. The first hole went into wet sand. Nothing to it. On the next hole I hit rocks. The shovel was no help, and neither was the posthole digger. I'd brought along a one-pound coffee can to remove what the posthole digger could not. The rocks laughed my can to shame. Even with Dennis's bar, it took the rest of the afternoon to dig two sorry little postholes. I can't even call them holes in good conscience. They were more like dimples, about as wide at the top as they were deep and lined with very little in the way of anything that could hold a post, mostly river cobbles.

On Sunday I tried again. Dennis McKeever had a standard excuse for working on a Sunday: "It says in the Bible that when your ox gets stuck in the mud on a Sunday you should go ahead and pull him out. Well I don't have an ox, but the way things have been going, if I did, it'd be stuck sure as hell."

It didn't take me long to figure out that you can't dig through rocks. You have to dig around them. For the little rocks, say fist-sized or smaller, I worked on my knees with a three-foot wrecking bar, wedging it against a rock and wiggling it loose until I could pull it out by hand. If that didn't work I'd stand up and pry it out with the big bar. I never knew how big a rock I'd hooked until it was landed. Some of the little rocks behaved like big rocks. Whenever I hit a big rock that wouldn't budge, I was tempted to start a new hole to one side or the other, but in that gravel I'd be likely to hit a bigger rock still, or a ruined civilization, and wish I'd stuck with the old hole.

When I was a boy we used to visit my dad's folks on the farm in Delaware. It was foreign country to me. That Sunday morning, working on my knees, fingernails torn, hands rubbed raw from clawing pebbles out of the ground, I remembered two things my father had told me about Delaware. He said you could walk into the melon patch on a hot summer afternoon, break a whole water-melon on the ground, and eat it right then and there, in handfuls. And he said that there were no rocks in Delaware.

I could forget the fence altogether, sell the sheep, and lose an investment of five holes; I could keep digging; or I could move to Delaware. Too stubborn to sacrifice those five holes, I decided to keep digging.

That afternoon Molly shouted down to me in the field. The neighbor had called to say he was done with the water and it was my turn to irrigate. I dropped the bar, pulled on my irrigation boots, broke the neighbor's dams, and flooded the field. I let the water run all that week, until the ground was good and soaked, and then I let the water run some more. My five postholes filled up with water. I leaned on the shovel and watched the clouds. Then one morning I remembered the sheep in their pen and the high price of hay. I put the water back in the river and started to dig again.

The fenceline cornered near an anthill. I finished one hole and started another before the ants, the biting kind, discovered me. Whether they took me for an enemy or whether they wanted to loot my piles of gravel for roofing tile, I can't say. As I grubbed in the hole, I constantly had to brush them away. Even at that, one of the little buggers got through and bit me on the neck.

The digging did not improve. It dawned on me that afternoon that I was trying to plant my fence in the middle of an extinct river-bed. The river had shifted into its present course and sentenced me to digging postholes in rocks. Nobody should be made to do such a thing. And the funny thing was, nobody was making me do it. The job had already taken on an urgency and a meaning that had very little to with its original goal, putting in a fence to pasture the sheep. No, it was man against nature now.

I was working under a pair of lofty broadleaf cottonwoods, and in spite of everything, enjoying their company. Cottonwoods don't generally live any longer than people. I'd been feeling more mortal than usual since I started building the fence, and these two trees, man and wife, had been sharing in that sense of mortality. A kingfisher landed in one of them, spotted the man kneeling in the field, and took off again, clattering. Anything that can fly as straight as a kingfisher must know what it's doing. Compared to his purposes, mine seemed hopelessly circuitous.

Molly had asked me to keep an eye on Hannah, our daughter, ten months old, playing in front of the house some twenty undug postholes from where I was working. So I turned my back to the river and looked up from my hole now and then to locate her small

[83]

head. There she was, peeking into the cage where we kept the ducklings. I nudged a rock with the digging bar. It wouldn't come. I found a smaller rock above it and pulled it loose with my fingers. It was the key to the larger rock. Hannah, elbows dug into her ribs, was toddling towards the house. I reached into the hole almost to the shoulder to remove the loose sand. A sudden wind came from the village. It had the screams of little girls in it. Four crows flew up, detonated from the ridge beyond the house. The wind bent the willows, but it did not tear at me like the lunatic wind of Arroyo Seco, where there was nothing, not a tree to stand in its way. It was a summer blow, the kind that comes before rain. Dennis's bar hit a big rock. There was no way around it. That hole was deep enough anyway. I picked up and moved to the next.

That night my boss at the block plant called to say he had a good deal on a semi-load of Mexican cement that had been delivered from El Paso. The driver crossed the border without paying duty and somehow managed to miss all the weigh stations going north in his badly overloaded Peterbilt, and so the good price. The boss asked me if I could come back to work in the morning.

"I sure need the work, Jerry," I told him, "but not unless you can give me a raise."

"How much of a raise?"

"How does four-fifty an hour sound?"

"Four-fifty an hour? You must be kidding. I'm the boss and I only make five."

I wanted to say that was his problem, not mine. Instead I said something about how I was right in the middle of building a fence and how finishing it had become a matter of dire necessity, if not honor. When I hung up, I thought of that sign behind the counter in the Abiquiu mercantile: "Why work 8 hours a day for someone else when you can be your own boss and work 15?"

The wind was blowing again in the morning even before the day warmed up. I was getting closer to the ditch, and once I reached it I'd be out of the field, digging in the shelf of earth where the house stood. Even right below the ditch, the rocks didn't seem to be getting any smaller or fewer. I spent the morning studying their shapes in the ground and grappling them free, the easy ones and the ones that wanted to be left alone. After I'd been looking at nothing but the ground for fifteen minutes or more at a time, the sky looked abnormally blue.

By early afternoon I was at and past the ditch. The rocks changed into sand, and then, in the next hole, to soft black dirt. I already knew this dirt. I'd dug my foundation trenches in it. It was the first dirt I had ever come to know very well, during a snowy Easter week when I took cover from the squalls in a trailer parked in the same rocky pasture that was about to get fenced in; when at every break in the storm, I hurried out to dig a little more before the snow started again. At the time, I found nothing much to love about this dirt. It wasn't anything like the dirt they had in Delaware. Once you got down a few inches it was caked with caliche and stuck to any tool that touched it, so you constantly had to be scraping off your shovel. This time, it was a piece of cake. Angelfood.

I put the wrecking bar aside and found the posthole digger, still standing in the willows at the river crossing where I'd given up on it. Now I could work standing up, like a human being, using Dennis's bar to loosen the dirt and the digger to lift it out of the hole. The wind blew harder than it had earlier, but by now I was moving into the lee of the house. I was digging a hole near the black locust when I spotted a large bird of prey across the valley, maybe an eagle, soaring close against the mountain. It dropped out of sight into the trees, but a few minutes later a crow chased it back into view, and then another crow, the two of them chasing the eagle south along the tops of the trees. They seemed to enjoy their work. They enjoyed it even more because of that brutal wind, which only their kind can fully appreciate.

Two days later I had dug my holes, set my posts, and was stretching field wire with a bumper jack. Dennis McKeever came looking for his digging bar.

"Well, Tom, did it do the job for you?"

"Dennis," I said, "that old bar couldn't dig a hole in a snow drift. I had to dig most of those rocks out by hand, and it took me the best part of two weeks to do it. The thing is, I want to build another fence down along the ditch one of these days. I'm thinking if you still wanted to sell me this bar, I could make do with it until I can afford a new one. How much are you asking for it?"

He hemmed and hawed.

"Well, Tom, you're right, this bar isn't everything it could be. One of these days I'm going to take it downtown and get a good edge ground on it. I'm going to have them straighten it out, too, and weld a little plate on this end, see, so you can tamp with it. Understand, you being a neighbor and all, I wouldn't want to sell you anything but the best."

THE GREAT BLUE HERON, *ARCHAEOPTERYX,* AND THE THROWBACK CHICKEN

> He felt again the old stab of wonder — what structure of
> life bridged the reptile's scale and the heron's feather?
>
> — Eudora Welty, "A Still Moment"

Seeing everything, I'm in the habit of seeing nothing. If I'd been outside on that warm, snowy morning in mid-January, the heron would have appeared as a blue blur in a landscape of blue blurs, a rock or a clump of willows. But I was inside taking a bath, and the frame of my bathroom window made visible what otherwise would have stayed ghostly and unseen.

A squall covered the hills. Just as I stepped out of the tub I saw him — a gaunt, hunched, brooding shadow among the willows of the beaver pond. Meat eater. Lover of swamps and waterways. He stood there for a while; then he tried to fly: *tried* because the first wingbeats were so stiff, so labored, that it might have been the effort of some primeval animal, struggling against its nature into a birdless atmosphere, as if the idea of flight, potential for ages in the genes of ancestors, had suddenly flared up in him. The long, snaky neck reached for something to grab. The degenerate wings drove him upright. Then as I stood there toweled and shivering, my same old amphibious self, he changed into a bird, flew solemnly, heavily over the clean white fields and the bent skeletons of sunflowers, into snowfall, out of sight.

Imagine that in the time it took for the water to drain out of the bathtub, I witnessed an event that in fact took millions of years — the ascendency of the birds on planet Earth. Like everybody, I'd heard that birds were the living kin of dinosaurs. Paleontologists have been telling us this on and off since the middle of the nineteenth century, but with new authority and zeal in recent years. No longer are dinosaurs the torpid, cold-blooded beasts I knew them to be as a child, when I marveled at those big glossy foldouts in *The World We Live In* (dismal, soupy landscapes; galleries of impossible gray beasts; pitiless world and time). Now we are being told that the dinosaurs, like the birds, were warm-blooded. They made their own internal heat. Like birds they moved around a lot and ate frequently. Their hearts beat at a good clip. They still couldn't fly, but given time, they would give rise and dominion to those who could.

None of this was important to me until the great blue heron struggled out of the river bottom that January morning. I was not exactly skeptical — just ignorant, in the sense of knowing little about the scientific findings, and in the sense of ignoring them, that is, not wanting to know. I couldn't make the wild leap between *Tyrannosaurus* — who had bones, but no flesh, whose awful, grinning presence in the Hall of Dinosaurs used to give me nightmares in the third grade — and those small, intense vegetarians, the hummingbirds. Rumors of the origin of birds first came to me at a time of my life when I was rejecting birds and flowers in favor of snakes, lizards, insects, worms, bacteria, molds, rusts, smuts — "eft things coarse" — things that lived under stones or inside of other things and made up the moist, rank, teeming, murderous life — the *real* life of our planet. I did not want to hear that birds were the living descendants of dinosaurs because it would have ruined my conception of them as ethereal beings, no blood to those of us who sweat and toil on solid ground. Birds were too visible. They were too beautiful. I wanted the hidden, monstrous truth.

At some point I realized I would not always have time to go peering into chuckholes and turning over rocks. Maybe beauty and visibility were all right after all. The birds flew by no matter what I was doing, strolling along the banks of the river or running a jackhammer. Yes, and birds were beautiful; in a world where beauty was not as common and accessible as I had once believed it to be, I thought I could learn to forgive them for that too. Their colors and speech began to turn my head, rescue me at work from blind fatigue. I found myself interrupting conversations ("Shhh! Hear him? Rufous-sided towhee.") and taken on summer evenings by flocks of violet-green swallows orbiting above the river. But who could find the dinosaur hidden in this picture?

The image of the heron kept coming back to me like a forgotten high school classmate in a dream, and with him, memories of other great blue herons. There was the one that preened near the bridge in eastern Oregon; one that startled me time and again on the Nueces in west Texas even though I knew where to find him and was expecting, even wanting to be startled; one that kept me awake on the Gila with its hellish, gutteral croaks, cries so strange that I could not tell whether they were being made by bird, beast, drunk, or broken machine until morning when I got out of the tent to look.

And my first. We were floating down the Colorado on a raft, a mile down from the top of the Grand Canyon gorge in an oven of black rock — the Vishnu schist, squeezed and cooked into its present chemistry two billion years ago. We'd just come through some rapids. His shadow crossed, and when I looked up, I saw the biggest bird I'd ever seen — hardly a bird at all, I thought — more like one of those Grade B monsters with leathery wings that abduct trolley cars. I watched his shadow slide across the green water and climb those unimaginably old rocks.

Years later I ticked off the great blue on my birdwatching life list. I also learned what I was supposed to have learned in grade school — that the grade-B monster, which had by then joined mice and ducks at Disney Studios, was a pterosaur, a flying reptile. Seventy million years ago the pterosaurs died out with the dinosaurs (natural history purges itself of melodrama; it used to be known as "The Great Death") but the birds — maybe because they sat on their eggs, waiting as faithfully as Horton to behold and love and feed their young instead of just laying their eggs in the sand and walking away in relief; and maybe because feathers gave them the secret of being small and warm-blooded at the same time — the birds lived on.

Then whose likeness had I seen in the January heron?

In Jurassic time, there lived a creature known as *Archaeopteryx* ("ancient wing") who for features both dinosaurlike and birdlike might have been dreamed up by a paleontologist trying to postulate a biological link between the two. He looked like a chicken with the head of a lizard — something from a book of composite beasts — a small terror, the size of a crow, a foot shorter than the shortest dinosaur and weighing no more than a pound. He had a set of file-like teeth, a long bony tail, and three claws on the end of each of his wing bones. Except for a naked head and a long, naked neck he was fully feathered and, structurally, those feathers were very like a heron's. In 1861 his fossil was spotted by a worker in the lithographic limestone quarry near Solnhofen, Bavaria. *Archaeopteryx* had come to rest on an ancient lake bottom in an attitude of troubled flight, his wings spread feebly, the rest of him all twisted and wrong. The fine silts and calcareous ooze of the lake buried him and produced in effect a lithograph, so finely etched that 130 million years later scientists could even make out the trace of a feather. If not for this one feather, they would have assumed the new animal to be just another Jurassic reptile, for no bird had yet been found in rocks that old; instead, they called it the first, the prototypical bird.

Or do we have to go back even further to log the first, to creatures even less beautiful than *Archaeopteryx? Sordus pilosus,* for example. A pterosaur whose name means "hairy devil." A batlike thing with three claws (again those claws) on its wings; a long snout for tweezing fish out of the water (like a heron's beak, and in fact, the whole head powerfully like that of another of our local carnivores, the belted kingfisher); a devilish spade on the end of its tail; and hair all over. Birdlike, maybe, but not a bird. *Sordus* could fly, but so can moths and bats; and even if those hairs of his are closer to being hairy feathers, as some have suggested, feathers alone do not make the bird. Robert T. Bakker has written that some of the small coelurosaurs (dinosaurs) probably had feathers too, although such frail, perishable things as feathers do not conveniently show up in the fossil to prove a point. No, a bird is a bird only because of the invisible configurations of its bones, and the way in which they fit together.

This was a hard lesson for me. Once upon a time birds had feathers and flew, nothing more. I was happy with those stunning flashes of yellow in this gray-green country, or a sad note in an aspen meadow. Somehow the sight of the great blue heron and questions raised by him about the ancient ones who lie printed in the rocks made my previous learning seem hopelessly inept. I knew how some birds looked and sounded, how still fewer behaved; but now, before I could know what they *were,* I was faced with the uncomfortable job of learning about their insides. I felt, on the one hand, somewhat corrupted by all this, reminded of a poem that makes a political distinction between looking at birds and studying them; on the other hand, elated by new kinds of mysteries, reminded of the wonder and absorption of a doctor friend who found the shambles of a cow skeleton and spent hours putting it back together ("Pass me that medial epicondyle over there, would you?"). So as I continued to live in the place most familiar to me of all places in the world — a place where the great blue heron appears rarely, a traveler and an outsider, I found myself in a strange territory, pondering the interior bird.

In the course of these wanderings I came on the hoatzin, a living South American bird, like our roadrunner, a member of the cuckoo family. The hoatzin builds its nest in a tree branch overhanging a river. Nestling young have claws on the ends of the second and third wing bones or "fingers" — as has been pointed out in the histories of birdlife — a lot like the claws on *Archaeopteryx.* When a predator threatens, the young hoatzin jumps out of the nest into the river, and when it's safe, swims to shore and claws itself back up into the tree.

This kind of behavior pleases me when I read about it in a book. The world is not such a tame, modern, predictable place after all. There are birds alive today, refugees from a dim past, who do not conform to my ideas of how they ought to look and act; who, instead of soaring and swooping, scratch and scrabble their way up the trunks of trees. I rejoice, as well, when I read that the great blue heron has been known to swipe goldfish out of suburban backyards, and at least once, a domestic kitten. (Man bites dog. Bird eats cat.) But every so often the wildness that I crave flies too close, makes me feel something other than the fondness of a man, safe and clean at his window, for the wild thing outside.

Not long ago I figured out that my twelve hens were giving me, on the average, half an egg a day. I fired up a pot of water and started the dirty work — lopping heads, letting them struggle inside a length of irrigation pipe to keep myself from getting dirty, dunking, plucking. I have an impression of them hanging there from a branch: bloody, headless, upside down, some feathered, some already plucked, a row of huge, primitive blossoms, a species that had resorted to such exotic means of reproducing itself that sex was hardly worth the trouble any more. I was almost done plucking one of the Barred Rock hens when I discovered a claw growing from one of its wings. Honest. A large, yellow, lizardlike claw.

Right here in my barnyard, tamest of all places, the hidden, monstrous truth had come to roost.

THE HOUSE AND ITS INHABITANTS

Twenty years had gone by since anyone lived in the Jaramillo house. Flickers broke nest holes in the wooden colonnade. Bat guano mounted in the attic, buried the ceiling joists, and caved in tinwork above the great hall. Shingles split and peeled away until the rain came in. The water seeped through the upstairs and washed gullies in the adobe walls. One room had melted entirely away, cantilevering an upstairs bedroom; and the rift in the drawing room would admit a cow, to say nothing of thieves, who had recently walked off with a carved mantel. It was decided the house would have to go.

People called it a shame. And as if that weren't enough to make me feel guilty, they might add, "I never expected *you* to be doing something like this." So to survive the job, I wore a mask of conviction. To see me in my hard hat, with my arsenal of wrecking bars, you would have thought "that man knows what he's doing and believes that it must be done," neither of which was entirely true. For starters, I was a builder, and this was a perversion of the trade. For the other, I knew that with ample time and money the house could be restored in place instead of taken in pieces for salvage. But what for? A reminder of lost grandeur in a poor town? And who, for the vastness of the place, for all its queer elegance, could ever feel at home there, or even welcome?

To wreck a house, as to build one, you must do one thing before the next. It's all backwards, but precisely backwards. So on the first day I was doing finish work—pulling trim and rolling up the embossed wallpaper — when Meg came to investigate, taking the stairs two at at time. She was about ten, very blond. She stood on the landing and watched as I broke a delicate length of molding, the kind used to hang pictures.

"You sure are making a mess," was her comment.

"Good," I said. "That's what I'm here for. If I'm making a mess, I must be making progress."

"What do you think you're doing, anyway?"

"Taking this old house down."

"You can't."

"Why not?"

"Because it's our hideout, that's why."

She wouldn't go away, just stood there, watching. To break the ice, I asked her how old the place was. She said it was built in 1880, but I didn't think it was quite that old, judging from the kind of nails coming out of it. But besides Meg, no one I had asked seemed to know for sure, and as an intruder, I kept the argument to myself.

"Three people were murdered here," she confided after a while.

"Sure hope I don't find any dead bodies."

"One in the kitchen, one in the stable, and one in that bedroom right over there," she said, pointing to a dark, rain-stained eastern corner where two barn swallows were raising a family.

"Are there any ghosts?" I asked.

"Oh sure. And there's a treasure hidden somewhere."

"If you find it, you have to give me half."

"No way, José," she said, and scampered back down the stairs.

At first I worked alone to keep breakage of the fancy woodwork to a minimum. As days passed I got clumsier, sometimes less than respectful. It was hard work, and lonesome. I had a few visits from Meg, and the company of the barn swallows, who whistled in and out through a broken window. They had built their nest of mud on the face of a brick chimney. Its open side was so close to the ceiling that even with a ladder I couldn't get high enough to see the nestlings. But I could hear them. During breaks I'd sit just outside the bedroom and watch the parents come and go. If I sat closer, they refused to enter the room. One night I looked in the bird guide to find out how long it would take for the young swallows to grow up and fly away. Too long. I'd have the roof off in a month. In a footnote, the book said, "Destruction of the barn swallow's nest is believed to bring harm — fire, lightning, death — to the house and its inhabitants."

A previous owner of the Jaramillo house said it had never been a hotel, although it was laid out like one. The central hall rose forty feet to a ceiling of painted tin panels, now rusted and abscessed by rainwater. A balcony ran four sides above the hall, and you could still read numbers on the bedroom doors. The entry, especially, belonged to an old-time hotel establishment: a stained-glass door; a vestibule partitioned by latticework; and in the center of this lattice, overhead, a large heart made of oak. "Home is where the heart is," I thought — a saying that implies homelessness, or a home away from home. A hotel. It was difficult for me to imagine anyone actually living in this house. Instead, I imagined negotiable women hanging on the balustrade above the gaming tables, the men and their cigars; steam and clatter from the kitchen; laughter flooding through a briefly opened door to meet, in darkness, the village's disapproval.

At the other end of the hall was what I took for the dining

room. A waysider had recently spent the night. He'd left behind some grape jelly, and it was sprouting little circuses of white mold. The dining room windows opened on the northwest, where across hayfields you could see a disintegrating adobe that looked as if it had been copied from the Jaramillo house: square, with a hipped roof; but instead of porches, a crippled outside balcony where the neighbors once sat and talked. In St. Louis, for example, the Jaramillo house would have been nothing very special; but in a ranching county of northern New Mexico, with millwork imported from then distant Golden, Colorado, it must have been something to talk about.

From the dining room, if you climbed the stairs (the treads not yet badly worn and still holding the concave tin triangles that once made it easier for a maid to sweep out the corners) to one of the bedrooms, you could climb a ladder into the attic and another ladder to the very top of the house, a flat deck abbreviating the severe pitch of the roof. Standing there with the four chimney stacks, you stood above everything in El Rito except the water tower at the vocational school. A woman who grew up near El Rito remembers the summers of her youth, when the guests of the house would come out on this deck to take the evening air. She said they looked like birds, gathered there above the town, strung along a wrought iron railing that had long since fallen away.

Hidden from the road by cottonwoods and box elders, Meg and her older sister turned the front yard into military headquarters. They nailed a few boards in the branches of the biggest box elder for a lookout, and sculptured the yard with their war apparatus: ropes, broomsticks, buckets, picnic benches, and a lean-to; this last, a rotting door that had been put over the well to keep chil-

[98]

dren and animals from falling in. Whenever I had business near headquarters, I had to endure the silent rage of the sister, much worse than if she had spit at me and called me a housewrecker. I never did learn her name. She never spoke directly to me, making her feelings known through her liaison officer, Meg. But why should she have spoken to the man who was spoiling things?

One day I was crawling in the plum thicket recovering bricks from a toppled chimney when the two girls approached, whispering.

"Ask him," said the sister.

"Did you take our ladder?" asked Meg.

"If you mean the one that goes to the attic, yes, I took it. It belongs to the house."

"Tell him to bring it back," said the sister. "Tell him we need it to get up into our treehouse."

I said I'd put it back when I was done with it, but I never did. Determined to get the house down before winter, I forgot how it had felt to be eight years old and see my own hideout obliterated for a New York housing project.

With the upstairs trim removed, I began to strip the pine tongue-in-groove from walls and ceiling, popping one nail at a time: lovely golden boards, nearly free of knots. Why would someone cover them with wallpaper? I bared the bones of the house until with ceilings down, tubes of sunlight pierced the old gloom. I was becoming familiar with my forebears, the carpenters. I saw their measurements and blueprints penciled on the backs of boards. In my backwardness, I loved their loose joints and hated their tight ones. Often, where one nail would have been enough, they had driven three, and I felt they were hanging around the place to poke fun at me as I fumed and swore, trying to undo what had been so well done.

I saved the swallows' room for last. At first, one or the other would fly in with a bug for the nestlings and at the sight of me, loop instantly back out the window. As I worked, they got bolder, sometimes hovering frantically by the nest, but never landing. They'd fly out again to rest on a power line until drawn in again, helpless to stay away. I left the boards on the ceiling, hoping that the young ones would learn to fly before their time and save themselves from me.

About this time I got a helper, and we went to work on the downstairs door and window frames, freeing trim to get at critical nails and extracting frames whole from two-foot-thick adobe walls. There were times, with my nose in a rat's nest, probing for the buried head of a finish nail, when I wanted more than anything to walk away and let the weather finish the work it had begun. Once I blundered into a hive of bumblebees above the front door, and thinking they were after me, took an early lunch. They were still stirred up when I got back, their chambers now open to the light where I'd pried a trim board loose. But when I tore the hive apart with the claw of a wrecking board, they only drifted into walls and against the woodwork, utterly lost.

The last frame to go was the one that held the wooden heart. I worked an entire morning to cut it away from the walls and balcony, leaving the whole thing in one piece — frame, latticework, heart. Taking it apart would have ruined it. Four men carried it out through the dining room. With the back wall knocked out and the frame tipped on the diagonal, we barely cleared the adobe on either side. No door would be wide enough to admit it again: its new house, wherever that might be, would practically have to be built around it. With a sense of ceremony, we loaded it on a flatbed truck and stored it in an oak grove a few miles up the valley.

With the heart gone, and nothing much left inside that could be damaged, we started on the roof. For three hellish days we swung sledgehammers to loosen strapping from the rafters. From top to bottom, we pushed the rubble ahead of us until it fell to the ground or snagged in the trees; once full of plums, they now grew a crop of cedar shingles. Each day we went home black, as if we had just finished a shift in a coal mine, for over the years the shingles had trapped soot from the house fires, and each blow of the sledge brought it down on us. The place looked bombed, and we were its few burnt survivors, looking for something to save out of the wreckage.

It was too much for the swallows. The morning after we started to demolish the roof, I found three young birds dead on the floor below the nest, sacrificed by the terrorized parents. The adult swallows never came back, and after they left, it was only a job. Even the magnificent blue hornets who lived under the eaves could not console me. Meg and her sister still played in front, but it was too dangerous for them inside. I could hear their playacting when the hammering stopped: the deranged general, his incompetent aide.

Note: The home of Venceslao and Cleofas Jaramillo was completed in 1900 and torn down in the summer of 1979. Its last owner applied unsuccessfully for public assistance to have it restored.

SHOOTING THE WELL

The welldigger couldn't quite understand why anyone would want to live so far away from anything and anybody, but supposed that was none of his business. Everybody had to be somewhere, right? And as long as you had to be somewhere you might as well be where there was lots of water. Even before he started drilling, he allowed that I was "in" the river, meaning I was directly on top of the part that ran underground. "In" or "over" was a distinction of little significance to a welldigger. If you wanted water, all you had to do was dig down and get it.

On the afternoon of the second day, he was baling out my new well. "Twenty GPMs," he said, "give or take." Gallons per minute, that is. More water than I was ever likely to have use for. He cut these little slits into the casing as it went down. "Perforations," he called them, a word I became very familiar with in months to come, rattling it off knowledgeably to plumbers and pump dealers and chemical supply clerks and neighborhood water witches, along with other words I learned to use, not always fondly, when speaking of my well.

The finished well casing stuck about a foot out of the ground. The welldigger welded a little steel plate on top of it so nothing could fall down in there that shouldn't, like rats. I'd never seen any rats in that part of the country, but supposed that was none of my business. As soon as the welldigger packed up his drilling rig, got paid, and left, I knocked the plate off with a sledgehammer and looked down inside to see what I'd just shelled out a thousand dollars for. Sure enough, there it was: the river, no more than twelve feet underground. Just before leaving, the welldigger had taken a certain perverse satisfaction in pointing out that "a body" — not his, to be sure — could have dug that far with a shovel.

For all my GPMs, I still didn't have any way to get the water out of the ground. The welldigger had said that most things in life — cars and marriage, to name only two — give only as much as you put into them. A water well, on the other hand, gives as much as you take out. Just digging a well isn't enough. You have to "develop" it, that is, you have to pump water out of it. If you do, the secret underground arteries will open up; the water, being a creature of habit, will feel loved, and respond generously. If you don't, things will start to close up, fill in, choke off. The water will find someone new.

This wasn't exactly what the welldigger told me, but my best understanding of the situation. I admit to being a little superstitious about these things. What if (as a friend once suggested) western civilization had violated the laws of nature by putting water in pipes? Had I sinned, violated the earth by driving a steel stake into her heart? What about forcing the water up out of the ground into the confinement of PVC, ABS, galvanized, and copper, when the nature of the element is always to spread out and go down? Was I going to get it in the end?

Never mind. There was a new baby in the house, diapers to do, and no water to do them in. If not for the baby, I could have found any number of reasons not to develop my well (like the neighbor who let his adobe house go unplastered year after year, as he explained, so the wasps would have plenty of time to drill holes in it, and the plaster would hold better). But the baby's grandmother stubbornly maintained that a house with a baby in it must also have water. Before the frost, I borrowed a hand pump and started developing.

The water in my well was opaque. If you filled up a bathtub with it and put your goldfish in, you would not have been able to see them. It looked like water that had been standing for a long time in a horse trough, in a pasture without any horses. It was orange, and turned things in its vicinity orange: T-shirts, porcelain sinks, fingernail cuticles, the teeth of goats. If allowed to settle, it would precipitate an orange slime on the bottom of the bucket — whether animal, vegetable, or mineral, nobody knew. It tasted funny, too, although in time, I came to accept it as the taste of home, and all other water, city water in particular, tasted bland and lifeless by comparison. It occurred to me that it might have something awful in it, but the house was so far away from other people or industry of any kind I couldn't even imagine what the awful thing might be. It left an orange scale wherever it sat for a long time, such as on the electrodes of my daughter's vaporizer. Over the years, working from the inside out, would it slowly turn me into a man of steel?

In a test tube, the water looked even more pathogenic — my own diseased blood, I fancied, on its way to unemotional strangers for the fatal diagnosis. No surprise, the laboratory reported that my water had high concentrations of iron, among other minerals; but also of harmless bacteria that fed on iron in solution. Millions of invisible creatures not only accepted this water, but feasted, thrived on it. I was determined to do likewise.

"The system" lived up to expectations for a while after the electric pump and pressure tank were installed, bountifully watering hedge roses and garden. But towards the end of that first summer, contrary to the welldigger's law of hydrodynamics, the well started to go dry. The more I pumped, the less I got. The water would run encouragingly for a while, say ten or fifteen minutes, followed by violent rumblings in the pumphouse. A sound like the universe getting sucked back into its original state of nonexistence: the big bang in reverse. In the garden, the hose would stop running, lie horribly still for for a few seconds, twitch uncontrollably, hemorrhage a small quantity of thick orange fluid, and die.

Neighbors advised me that the groundwater level was falling, and that I would have to go to "second water." The welldigger could probably put me in second water by punching the well casing down maybe another hundred feet at, say, twelve dollars a foot, but with no guarantee he would end up with anything more than a dry hole. I decided to diagnose the problem on my own. Lowering a pipe elbow into the well on the end of a string, I found that the water had not fallen so much as an inch. Twelve feet down it had started and twelve feet down it remained, arranging itself as comfortably and inevitably in the ground as the molecules in a crystal.

"Have you checked your intake?" the welldigger asked on the telephone.

I had not. My intake was a metal cone with holes in it at the bottom of the well, where water first entered the pipes. It might be getting buried by a slow accumulation of sediment, or the holes might be getting clogged with something or other (in my homeowner's nightmares, something alive and purposely malignant), and the only way to find out was to pull the pump and take a look.

My intake came out black and crusty, but the holes were open, and as far as I could tell, nothing was blocking the free and limitless passage of water. I shined the metal up with a wire brush, cut off two feet of pipe in case the intake was getting mired, and tried again. No luck.

"Sounds like your perforations are closing up," said the welldigger the next time I called. He said that happened a lot, especially around where I lived, where the water was so hard you could stand a spoon in it. If my perforations were closing up, the only thing to do was agitate. He said the minerals in the water were probably getting deposited in those perforations, sort of like barnacles, I imagined, so that even when the water kept its level when fully recovered, it was coming into the well at a slower rate. He said he could agitate for me, but when I heard how much it would cost, I decided I could agitate for myself.

My agitator was a piece of metal lath fashioned into a kind of basket and attached to the end of a twenty-foot length of reinforcing bar. I jammed it down in the well one afternoon and agitated for all I was worth. I agitated until I was good and tired of it, and then I agitated some more.

"Acid," said the welldigger, when I reported that agitation had failed. "Sulfuric acid. If that doesn't work, nothing will."

The acid came in bite-sized yellow pellets, like one of those newfangled animal feeds, only this kind of pellets cost about fifty dollars a gallon bottle. The manufacturer said it was just the thing for rejuvenating crusty old wells (I didn't admit that mine was a crusty new one), and that judging from the depth of the well and the hardness of the water, I would need two gallons.

One afternoon, per directions, I pulled the pump. I was getting to be an expert at pulling the pump. It was like extracting a long shiny black worm from the throat of a sick dog, only more difficult. Then, still following directions, I dumped both bottles of acid into the well at once. Sure enough, just as predicted, you could hear it working down in there. You could smell it, too. Brimstone. The retributive fires of hell. Just like a giant alka-seltzer. At last, science had taken command.

Twenty-four hours later, the acid had fizzed itself out, and I turned on the water. It came out black and smelly, and in no greater quantities than before. I stopped giving it to the chickens — an unnecessary precaution, come to think of it, since even a chicken would have had better sense than to drink it — and began hauling water from the river for dishes and baths. The local mercantile supplied my drinking water, five gallons at a time. For some reason, the faucet came up out of the floor right in the middle of the aisle, between the Fritos and the Cheerios, so I had to put up with the knowing looks of townspeople every time I went to town for a refill. One evening, feeling rebellious, I took a long drink out of the barrel with riverwater in it. It tasted disturbingly familiar; in fact, exactly like my well water, before its corruption.

At last, it wasn't science that saved the well, but a scientist — a new neighbor, and like all new neighbors, regarded by the community with a combination of curiosity and distrust, as well as the feeling that anyone foolish enough to move as far away from everything as that deserved whatever they got. My neighbor was a computer scientist, a troubleshooter, often disturbed in the middle of the night and summoned over great distances to get one computer or another back on its feet. He and his wife wanted to build a house by the river, a little downstream from where I had built mine. More foolishness. The mosquitoes would eat them alive in July, and during floods, the river had been known to come up over their planned homesite. But it was a comfort to find someone in the neighborhood even greener than I, who also had the bad sense to think he could build a house, and dig a well, and be happy. At first, I pretended to be an authority on domestic water systems, telling him all the things he should and should not do when he dug his. But after a couple of beers, feeling in the presence of a kindred spirit, I broke down and told him the whole painful history.

"Why don't you shoot it?" he wanted to know. And, being a neighborly sort, he offered to shoot it for me.

So one afternoon in August, when the sunflowers and asters were out along the fencerows and the goldfinches were singing the way they do that time of year, and everybody was eating corn and cutting hay and beginning to get in some wood for the winter, and the world in general seemed a more hospitable place than it had at certain other times, he showed up at my house with a .44 magnum, climbed down the ladder into the wellhouse, plugged his ears, and fired four rounds into the astonished open mouth of my well. Someday, he promised, he was going to try it on a computer.

As if by magic (and for my money, there was far more magic in it than physics), the water leapt forth. From then on, I could run the well all day long and never run it dry. The water was as hard as ever, to be sure, and continued to stain me, my loved ones, and much of what I owned orange. But there was plenty of it — more than enough to do the diapers and water all the young apple trees at the same time.

Later that year, I had to order a new set of points for the pump motor (the old ones had worn themselves out sucking air), and not to tell the welldigger his business or anything, mentioned how I'd finally solved my problem.

"Yeah," he conceded. "That'll work. But dynamite's even better."

WILLOWS

It started with the worms, or what looked like worms, and spread from one clump of willows to the next all along the river. If I had noticed it back in the days when it was getting its start, I did not recognize it as anything foreign to the plant, certainly not as anything deadly. There are many kinds of willow. Maybe this one had a strange kind of bark; not smooth, like the small, weedy variety, the common one, that shot up all along the ditches and water-courses, but bumpy. Maybe I saw the bumps and thought "lenticels" — thin, horizontal pores, like wounds almost healed, that distinguish the bark of the water birch, for example; and such a beautiful word that I would have thought it, said it, written it at the slightest provocation, no matter if they were lenticels or not. Maybe I thought "lenticels" and went on about whatever had brought me to the river — work, or more often, the need to get away from work and be by the river. Then again, maybe I didn't see them at all, or saw them and thought nothing of them. Willows grew everywhere in the perennially wet places; couldn't be stopped from growing. It was easy to take them for granted.

Most of them occupied the low fringe of the riverbank, a strip of sediment that they depended on for a foothold and that probably would have washed away in the spring floods but for the stabilizing, binding presence of the willows. Once established, they broke the river's velocity at its edge and robbed it of sand and mud, making ground for young willows. I came to believe they were the single unchanging fact of the riverbank. Everything else changed in their neighborhood, not just over a long time, but quickly, perceptibly, and sometimes catastrophically. You could hear beavers chewing on the cottonwoods at night, in the days before they cut down all the trees on the near bank of the Servilleta. Once, on a day without wind, I saw one of those trees fall. The bank changed too, always getting torn down over here and built up over there. I'd find a special place to sit and flip rocks into the water, then when I looked for the same place another time, it would be gone, or too well disguised to be special the way it had been before.

But the willows hung on. Flooded, they held fast where a less flexible tree might have lost its grip and fallen. If standing in the way of enough water, the willows might lie down under the weight, stripped of every leaf and smothered by river trash; but when the flood was over, they would still be there, bending over in the shiny new mud. They had an uncanny grip on life, always taking exception to weakness and mortality. Cut off at ground level and stuck in the moist sand, they thrived. Mowed down with a tractor, they came right back up again. They were too limber to break and too thoroughly creatures of water to burn. A bulldozer would leave them skinned and splintered, but nothing short of taking half the riverbank out would finish them.

In the spring, their colors came out with snow or rain: some yellow, some plum red. Two different species? It annoyed me that the difference required an explanation. Wasn't it enough that there was color in the world to be seen and enjoyed? Why did people have to go and ruin things by trying to understand them, and even worse, to classify them? But there they were, hopelessly tribal. Through the years at La Junta, my sense of the difference between yellow willows and red ones grew clearer. But the disease made no such distinction, treating all alike.

I used to go for river walks down the Vallecitos, meandering through willows. Not too many cows and almost no people went there, mainly mice, rabbits, skunks, raccoons, beavers, snakes. Coyotes came down off the mountain to drink and maybe grab a chicken out of somebody's yard. Hordes of redwinged blackbirds took over the willow thicket in the spring — the males hunched up in that gimpy display, pouring out music the way only blackbirds know how to pour it, flashing red, the color of passion. Small yellow blossoms appeared on the willows when it got warm — humble flowers, and from any distance, nothing more than a dusting, an intuition of yellow. Multiplying as effortlessly as they did, what need did they have for show? Here and there the walk led across other people's property, through hummocky, pissy, cowed-out pastures, but it was easy enough to keep under the cover of willows to keep from being seen. Not that anyone would have cared that I was trespassing, but for a little while, I wanted to be entirely alone and invisible, and not even have to imagine, much less to give, an excuse for being there.

It was a great place for hiding. The willows grew bigger and more thickly on the Vallecitos than on the Servilleta, and at their thickest, it was next to impossible to get through. A calf separated from its mother might find itself coralled and bawl until its eyes bugged out. The cows made trails, but those only went where cows did, so if I wanted to go anywhere else I'd bushwhack or crawl. The willows grew in clumps, and the space between them widened towards the ground into cool alleyways where the sunlight was broken up but never entirely shut out and the mud smelled good enough to eat. In this sanctuary, if I had a mind to, I could move among willows without getting whipped in the face, unobserved except by whatever was crawling around in there with me. Birds landed close by, sometimes right overhead. The small, delicate shapes of clawed feet were printed there, and the grass lay down along customary ways. Here, one of the residents had built a monument of perfect, gleaming turds. Here, they had slept. There were places among the willows that were hard to recognize as distinct when I walked upright, wading blindly through miniature counties and municipalities. As children, we went around the house with mirrors under our chins, carefully stepping over ceiling fixtures and archways, hanging deliriously upside down like flies. Like crawling through willow thickets, it was a way of changing perspective.

I went on these walks with the assumption that there was an unknown destination or event waiting that would be recognized when the time and the place came. There might have been many other sightings along the way, coming or going, but the most significant one, the turning point, could not be mistaken or missed. This recognition went both ways, and with it came the feeling that each of us had been traveling towards the other. It might pass as quickly as a man holding a lantern in the dark, seen from the window of a moving train; or it might last long enough for lying down and dreaming. Once the instant or the hour passed, there was a sense of completion. Gravity called the thrown object back to earth. Even if I kept walking in the same direction, the walk led irrevocably home.

Many such destinations were concealed among the willows, making theirs an especially dear neighborhood, a place to be visited instead of just lived in (lived-in places have a way of disappearing to those who live in them, in spite of best efforts to keep them from fading out of sight; so people travel). At La Junta, a barbed wire fence strung at the far side of the near pasture and running roughly parallel to the Servilleta was the arbitrary dividing line between places to be and places to go. Willows were left to grow as thick as they liked on the other side of the fence. Trespassers got yanked out of the garden in their infancy or mown down in the field, but the other side of the fence belonged to them. The fence separated the world of people, including the animals and plants who depended on people for their survival, from the one that would get along fine without us. In this other world the substances of earth, water, plant, and flesh could be observed or not observed without conscious reference to human livelihood; although in a literal, biological sense, I could not have lived without it. Observed, the inhabitants of this world could not escape my habit of naming them: this is a rock; a round rock; a pink, round rock. Unobserved, it was still enough that they existed, uncorrupted by attempts to call them this or that, and graciously, forever capable of being seen if I took a notion to see them.

An ancient stone wall ran down one side of the driveway and across the far side of the lawn at my aunt and uncle's place in Connecticut, forming the border of the cultivated part of their property. This wall was much admired and talked about through the years. The ground was so full of rocks in Connecticut, it was explained to us children, that the people who originally farmed the place had to pick them out of the ground by hand when they plowed and stack them up at the edge of the field. Adults never made clear what these homesteaders wanted to do more — get rid of the rocks or make a wall — but given the practical nature of farm people everywhere, it could be assumed they wanted to do both.

It was a beautiful wall, made not of pink, round rocks, but of coarse, black ones, forged in Precambrian furnaces, if not in the fires of hell. Unlike the stone walls of houses and barns in New England, most of which were made to stand up forever, this wall looked as if it had been thrown together by people who had other things to do besides making a wall and didn't really care how well it stood. It had the special beauty of things not made to last. If you climbed on it, you had to be careful because the rocks could shift and fall. Climbing was generally discouraged, as much for the sake of the wall, which was precious and destructible, as the safety of the children. Moss grew on it in places, and vines of different sorts, and the stones were stacked loosely enough that small animals, chipmunks and squirrels, could go in and out. The wall separated our world, that of barbecues, croquet, and gently enforced appreciation of Roy and Nancy's plantings, from the world of mystery, danger, and wildness that lay beyond: one we could visit and wonder about, even if we didn't belong there.

When we arrived from the city, Roy would stop his mowing long enough to greet us. His was an enormous, lumpy lawn, made not by grading and seeding or by rolling out carpets of sod, but by mowing. If you mowed an open piece of ground often enough and kept the water on it, he explained, eventually it would turn into a lawn. But you had to keep after it, or the weeds, and sooner or later the forest, would move back in, and things would be the way they had been before the farmer came and cut down the trees and built the wall. We gathered that wonderful as it was, wild nature was allied with weedy lawns and other forms of anarchy, and rightly belonged on the other side of the fence.

So we had to go there to see it. Nancy, who had long since given up trying to be known by her real name, Anna Katharine, led these expeditions in her galoshes, often tying a scarf around her head under a straw sunbonnet. It was marshy down below, and there was the constant menace of poison ivy. If we had worn shoes that shouldn't get wet we could borrow a pair of galoshes from the dark garage, pantheon of Roy's lawnmowers, always smelling of cut grass and gasoline. The croquet set was kept there, idle between visits: the heavy wooden balls nesting in their separate holes, each one parented by a mallet of like color; and the wickets, convalescent with little strips of bedsheet tied to them. The galoshes felt strange; many sizes too large, and hot. I could feel the ground through them, and deep mud sometimes sucked them right off my feet.

My aunt, intrepid, led us through the gate — three poles bridging a gap in the wall and always replaced behind us, a habit learned when there had been cows to get in, and practiced long after the farms had turned to suburbs. She had been known to shoot woodchucks from an upstairs window of the house. If not controlled, they would ruin the vegetable garden. We thought her grand for this, and never wasted any sympathy on woodchucks. ("Grand" was my grandfather's, her father's, word. "Isn't life grand?" he asked, meaning, without irony, that it was.) Woodchucks were about the only living thing my aunt ever spoke ill of, besides poison ivy; all else was praise and marvel. Along the way, she congratulated every thing that grew there for its life and health, or expressed sorrow for its failings. She knew them all by name.

Many of the names were Latin words, hard to pronounce and remember, but she said them in an easy, familiar way, as if saying the names of old friends. I probably got a lot of my compulsion to know the names of things from her. Through her interest in everything that was going on around her, she impressed upon me that the naming of a plant or animal magically allowed one to see it; yes, even to make it appear.

The path led through the shade of maples down the stone wall, which made a T at the gate. Here was Nancy's prized young redwood tree, a species native to a faraway part of the world and planted against local convention, but behind the wall where it would not cause any trouble. *Metasequoia* something or other. Her bees lived there too at one time, but if you kept going and were not afraid of them, they wouldn't bother you. Nancy had not always been dangerously allergic to bee bites and poison ivy, but loving to explore behind the wall and poke her nose into places where people did not ordinarily go, she got stung or infected too many times, weakening her immunities. Eventually, the kept bees had to go, and her reaction to poison ivy kept her on the mowed side of the wall on all but rare occasions. Once, burning a pile of weeds, she inhaled the smoke of this plant, and got poison ivy inside of her. This and a story from my father's side of the family about a great aunt who choked to death on a wheat straw first gave me the impression that the world out of doors, and especially on the other side of the wall, could be an ungentle place, where one organism could inflict injury on another without even meaning to. The inadvertent nature of this harm made it that much scarier.

It got wilder the farther down you went. In places, the path almost disappeared (a machete was also kept in the garage, and I was allowed to hack away down there when I got older), and the stone wall, overcome by vegetation, was sinking back into the ground. Mockingbirds spoke in local dialects. The pheasant, exploding from cover, made my heart skip a beat. There was every kind of bramble and thorn. Foxes, sighted from the house on rare occasions, lived in holes. Rafts of soft ground settled like a rowboat when you walked across them. Skunk cabbage. And finally, the creek, where it was always cool and shady in summer; where you could see turquoise and azure dragonflies ("darning needles," we called them, probably after the language of my father's more distant and mysterious side of the family) and catch frogs and minnows. I never went past the creek, and I don't remember whatever lay beyond being much spoken of — maybe someone else's property, or a road. If so, it was just as well left unseen, for in too close touch with the manufactured world, the one we had come from and were about to return to, our swamp would have lost much of its secrecy and terror.

The riverbank at La Junta, as a place of refuge from tameness and a place where the works of men and women were not encouraged, was akin to those few acres behind the wall at my aunt and uncle's place in Woodbridge. They planted Christmas trees to be harvested in a part of theirs; I longed to build a bridge across mine. But in both places, the implicit judgement of the owners was that some things are better left alone. It would have been nice to get equipment into the field across the river without getting stuck in the mud or to drive the sheep from one side to the other instead of dragging them through the water, but I came to believe that my survival at La Junta — that is, my ability to stay there in years to come — wasn't as important as observing what was going on from the perspective of a visitor; for instance, as a seven-year-old city boy visiting his relations in the country might observe them. The bridge would have made life easier, but if I'd wanted life to be easier, I wouldn't have moved to La Junta in the first place. What I wanted even more than a bridge was to sit on the grass among the immortal willows, watch the darning needles dive down over the water, and *think* about building a bridge.

One of those times, I began to understand that something was awfully wrong: those wormy bumps, or blisters, as if a great, sudden heat had passed, searing the bark of the willows and raising multitudes of tiny welts up and down the switches. Or like the larval stage of some insect, living on or under the bark, swarming over the body of the willow with the infinitesimal slowness of growing plants. I noticed that the willows on the near bank no longer came to life in the spring the way they had before, green and lush, swaying as luxuriously in wind as a cornbelt crop. They still pushed out shoots and leaves, but hesitantly, as if some kind of doubt had entered their existence. Clearing ground for a ram pen by the river, I noticed that some of them had gone dry and could be broken off, where normally, it would have taken an axe or a saw to get them out. And across the river, in a kind of hole or sink that caught the neighbor's irrigation water on my side of the fence, whole clumps of willows had died and stood clawlike and stiff, fooled into confident growth by the irrigation water, I guessed, then left high and dry.

It took a while to figure out that all the willows were sick, although in various stages of sickness; longer to guess that those swarms of maggot-like bumps were the cause of it, or at least the first symptom. The long axis of the bumps always went up and down the switch, so they all seemed to be going the same way and busy satisfying some common hunger, mocking the collective intelligence of an insect colony. But unlike insects, they didn't appear to move or eat or otherwise conduct themselves in a way that was at all natural. They had no nameable, placeable intelligence. They didn't exist in separate bodies, only in the communal body, and even that was borrowed, commandeered, rightly belonging to the willows. They came for no other apparent reason than to infect and kill, having no legitimate pleasure or ambition of their own; or having killed, to die, a murder-suicide. As far as I could see, there wasn't any redemption in them.

Over a time of seasons, then of years, it became apparent that what I had been thinking of as a "they" was really an "it." And the worst of it was, not having any feelings, it couldn't have them hurt. How can you punish a disease? For that matter, how can you even hate it? Maybe the spore of some deadly fungus had come on the wind, harmless to all others but the willows; or maybe the contagion had its origins in the ground, climbing up through the roots to feed on the willows from the inside out. But by the time the tokens of it had appeared, breaking out in insect legions, it was already too late. Within a year or two, the skin of the willow would be covered until it looked like the skin of a person who had caught some horrible cancer. Then the bark would split open and the willows would turn black and die, leaving nothing but the papery dead shells of willows all along the river.

A man from the county extension service came out one time, identified it as scale, and said not to worry, it probably wouldn't get on the apple trees. That was good news, but it was the willows that

I was worried about. I could have left them there, I suppose, to fall and rot in their own time, but it hurt to see them in that condition. I felt a little betrayed that they had gone and gotten sick in spite of all my admiration, in spite of all those glorious times we'd spent together on the riverbank, and in spite of the godlike strength and endurance I had imagined for them. Left standing, they were a reminder, too, of the unhealthiness in me, all those feelings of waste and failure that accumulate over the winter and have to be cleared away — buried, drowned, or burned — before there can be forgiveness and a starting over again. There were lots of other willows, healthy ones at that, up and down the valleys. The scale would never kill them all. Besides, where there had been nothing but dead willows, now there would be a place for the new grass to come up, and maybe even something as unprincipled as a cow.

So I decided to burn them. Stubborn to the last, they wouldn't burn in place the way they were supposed to, the way they did at ditch-cleaning time in La Chamita and El Guique: instantly, the whole riverbank consumed in glorious, reconciling flame. No, it wasn't going to be that easy. They would have to be gathered into piles first, like one of those miserable, impossible chores that can be performed only by the very clever or the pure of heart. Not being either of those things, I was going to have to go to work.

The scale had left the willows so brittle and substanceless that they wouldn't stand still to be cut with an axe. Most of them could be broken underfoot, though, trampled down until the decayed roots popped in the earth with a sound like bone tearing free of ligament. They came loose with a fist of lovely black riverbottom dirt still attached, which got knocked loose. Then they were dragged into piles for burning. Once lit, the piles refused to burn by themselves, and I had to stay there hour after hour, building new piles and feeding the unburnt ends of willows into the flames, and in spare moments, standing back to watch birds, clouds, and water — the kind of thing that had called me to the river junction in the first place and that justified invented kinds of work like clearing willows. They made a quick, hot flame and fell into ashes, and as they burned, the smell of their smoke came back to me from all the sickrooms, cafeterias, and Sunday evening fix-it-yourself suppers of my childhood: Campbell's chicken noodle soup.

It was the first week of March. The wind started to come up in the afternoons, and with it, the threat of a brush fire, so I built my piles in daylight and waited for a day of dead calm. The space on the riverbank grew like the inside of a house that someone was leaving. Sometimes it startled me to look down there and see those vagrant piles, the way a parking meter or a lamppost can strike you with its presence before the word for it comes to mind and it assumes its customary being and shape. I had grown so used to see-ing the riverbank as it had been that I would look and constantly have to look again, allow it to revise itself into the new thing.

The wind never did die down, not until late afternoons, any-way. The smart approach would have been to fire up the piles at dusk or dawn, ahead of or behind the wind. That probably would have been the way to go about it, but for some reason, I'd made up my mind that it had to be done in the stillest, but also the darkest and loneliest hours. It was a reckoning that had to be entirely between me and the willows, like shooting an old, sick dog. So I got up at about two o'clock one morning when there was no moon. It only took a little dry grass to get things started, then I stood back to watch as the flames spread and the circle of light widened. If anything, the firelight made it harder to see. It shut me into its circle and shut almost everything else out except the everlasting sound of the river, which was already giving signs of being on the rise, and for a while, the call of an Aztec owl: "tecolo, tecolo, o, o." He was somewhere across the river, maybe in that dead cottonwood by the spring, seeing in the dark. A single car drove by sometime during the night, slowed as it passed the fires, and speeded up again. A fire in the riverbottom in the dead of night meant witches. It was cold. When I got too close to the fire, the hair over my eyes shrank back from the flame and I could smell the burning hair, the way witches must smell when they burn. In the morning, my face would be as red as it got in deep summer, at hay time. The unburnt willows crowded into the flame and sent up sparks that rose and vanished, and the light would swell and show the shapes of things across the river. The light was a blessing, but it made me more vulnerable than I wanted to be, visible to all eyes at any distance. Once in a while I'd break away from the light and hide in the darkness like an animal, which made me feel safer, but then I'd get cold and have to go back in.

The house stood above me by the road, keeping its distance. I knew there was a place to sleep there, and food, but I wanted to be done with it once and for all, so I kept nursing the fires along, looking for daylight, and every once in a while, glancing up at the house like a thief. When daylight finally came, the water ouzel rejoiced in his place under the Vallecitos bridge, the way he did every morning. The hollow concrete cavern of the bridge amplified his voice to awful proportions. I threw on the last of the willows and watched them burn down to nothing.

After breakfast, I climbed the hill across the road and looked down. People were lighting house fires up and down the valley, and in the still morning, their smoke mixed with mine and sat on top of everything. The river looked pretty much the way it always did from up there, still gray-green in early March, except for that empty strip of riverbank where not too long before, the willows had grown so close that nothing else could grow among them, unless you counted the bastard cockleburrs, who didn't have any respect; but that now looked so tidy and hospitable, almost like a mown lawn. It was disturbingly like the ground on the other side of the fence, where the sheep were grazing. I told myself that everything was all right, that nothing could keep the willows from coming back once the disease had run its course. The river was beginning to stir. It was only a matter of weeks before it would quicken and break out of its confinement. Then new grass would come up in the black places where the willows had burned, and there wouldn't be any sign of what had happened.

MAGDALENA

And now we stare astonished at the sea,
And a miraculous strange bird shrieks at us.

— William Butler Yeats

May 11

Took a ladder down to the river to investigate a stick nest in a tree near La Junta. A magpie has been going and coming from there. Unusually close to the ground for a magpie nest, but branches made it next to impossible to reach without a ladder.

Eggs! Couldn't tell how many. Green, blotchy eggs! Magpie eggs! I'll steal a hatchling, raise it up for a companion, teach it to swear in Spanish.

May 16

Baby birds. Gray and pink, very soft and vulnerable, piled in their adobe bowl all on top of one another, so you can't tell what belongs to whom. Tadpolish at this age, five days at the most. They must have been ready to pop last week when I found the eggs.

No sign of eggshells either in the nest or on the ground. Does the mother eat them? The little ones were asleep, breathing. Before I climbed the ladder, it flashed on me that the mother might be there, sitting. Taking her place, I saw the huge, hairy, unbeaked head darken the treetops and peer into the privacy of my home.

[129]

Disconcerting.

Why do I want a magpie? Because they are beautiful and wise. Because they belong to that raucous, bullying, thieving race of birds, the corvids. Because they're kin.

I had a feeling there might be baby birds in the nest yesterday when I saw two adults near the tree instead of the customary one. But I'm new to this baby robbing business. When do you do it? When it gets its feathers? What do you feed it? Do you have to split its tongue to get it to talk? I want to know *everything* about magpies. Like Konrad Lorenz, eye-level in the pond with his beloved goslings. Will I go daffy, too? Hope so. I've been feeling much too sane lately, need something impractical. One of James Stephens's characters says when you're down in the dumps, find yourself something big and concrete to worry about. He buys a bull.

May 19
Can't get over this idea that the movements of people, their speech and actions, are pitiful and inconsequential compared to the movements that surround them — rivers flowing, insects scurrying, clouds burgeoning, birds flying.

June 1
I climbed the ladder to the nest, beheld not a mess of amphibious, scrambled-egg hatchlings, but a brood of young birds with feathers! They have grown incredibly fast. I took one. Magdalena? Or maybe Sheila. No way of telling its sex, but who cares? Since she's got to be one or the other, why not female? My partialities are showing.

Like the predator that I am, I had to break a hole in the nest to get my hand in. Now that it's done, I worry about consequences. What if the mother spurns the broken nest, abandons the rest of the brood? It's illegal to capture wild birds, isn't it? No help for it. This one's mine.

The mother flew into the tree as I was doing my dirty work, watched me closely, but didn't attack. One more or less, no big thing. The book says magpies will raise three or four broods a season if their nestlings are eaten or otherwise lost, but does that justify my taking a hatchling? It's nothing, I keep telling myself. But something here goes against my nature. I want so badly to regain my place as an inhabitant of the natural world — to prove that I belong in spite of my membership in the human species. But I'm a habitual outsider yet.

Saw the mother near the nest this morning. Maybe she'll overlook the loss.

June 2, morning
Puppy chow and water, the ideal magpie diet. Magdalena's nictitating membrane flashes at me like a camera shutter.

The secret of getting her to eat is to let her get hungry. No use trying to pry the beak open, it opens all by itself when it's ready. Already, she squawks at me to be fed; then when she gets it, satisfied little warbles. No tools required. Soak the food in the water, stuff it down her throat. The stuffing part took a little getting used to, because it really requires sticking my finger all the way down in there. That's how mama does, and that's how baby likes it.

The lining of her mouth, pinker than our privatest parts; the tongue, long, gray, and quick, like a lizard's.

Had to take her to work yesterday to feed her, captive in that rusty old no-bottom birdcage salvaged from the dump. Didn't know what I wanted it for until now. It's been cohabiting all these months with the used-up tires, a prince among paupers. This morning Hannah came to say that Magdalena was gone. What? Gone? Horror of empty birdcage: not so much that she's gone, but that you know for certain she was there just a minute ago. What you miss is not so much a baby magpie as your sense of how the world works. Things don't just disappear. They die and melt away, or get eaten, like that time-lapse film of a mouse carcass getting eaten by blowfly maggots (television is full of wonders). Found my magpie asleep behind the dresser.

Same night
Magdalena. Stimulus for change in my life. Renewal of awareness, badly needed.

June 3
Magdalena does not seem to know it's morning until she hears my voice. What they call "emotional attachment" is real. Love affair between man and bird. Or, better, man wishing to be bird.

June 4
With a magpie on my shoulder or on top of my head, I'm a new man. When she's on my head, nibbling at stray ends of hairs, I see things as a bird might see them.

I feel like a new parent again, four years after Hannah was born. Has it been four years already? Time accelerates with age. Something like fatherly love, anyway. To feel that love, and the child's or the bird's love in return, is a terrifying thing. Dependency and all that implies. With the first twinge of love comes the fear of losing the loved one.

Put Magdalena on the ground in front of the house last night, and she hopped into the hollyhocks. Fatherly concern. Will she be all right? No, it's not so much her safety that concerns me as keeping my possession of her intact. Infatuation, from the Latin *fatuus*, foolish.

She rode on my shoulder, claws dug in (nails? talons?). For the first time this year, it felt like a summer evening. Moving the sheep, I thought I spied the year's first grasshopper, a small one, but it will grow, and there will be others. I've read that magpies catch grasshoppers "with great agility," so I took her down to the corn garden, where I'd seen the hopper, and turned her loose on the ground. Awful decision. Do I clip her wings before she can fly, so she will always be mine, mine, mine; or do I let her fly, and risk losing her? Sentimental rotgut of all true-to-life animal adventures.

She followed me through the rows and stood within a few inches of the dog, who could have gobbled her up in one bite. No apparent fear. Will I have to teach her fear so when I turn her loose, she won't go off and get eaten? And this hair nibbling business — is that what the ornithologists call "allo-preening"? It says in the book that corvids (crows, ravens, magpies, jays) preen one another around the head and neck where their own beak will not reach.

Have to admit, it's pleasant. Pervert! Taking advantage of baby birds!

Hunger is the best salt. When she's hungry, she attacks my hand for the food it may or may not hold; when she's hungry but not so hungry, she throws her beak open wide, showing me the perfect red insides of her being, so wide that I am shy to look into it, for I may see things that I am not meant to see, the innermost innards of a living creature. I'm a poor substitute for a bird when it comes to feeding, but in the last few days, I've grown less squeamish. Parents can't afford to be squeamish. Now I shove my finger down in there like a regular mother, but not without the ghost of aversion.

June 5

Why teach a bird to talk? Better, learn *its* speech. In the old days, I'm told, a witch woman lived near here who, for a fee, would split your pet magpie's tongue, which is supposed to enable it to mimic the human voice. All corvids are great ventriloquists, but starlings have them beat. I heard one give a perfect imitation of a distant coyote while it was sitting on a telephone line directly overhead.

I'd rather hear what Magdalena has to say than hear what I say repeated. Begging cry. Warble of contentment and gratitude. A kind of wolf whistle. A raunchy squawk.

Dilemma. The people I've been working for want a magpie for an old lady friend of theirs who is losing the will to live. A hungry magpie would be just the thing to keep her on her toes, they say. Their magpies have already flown. Could they have one from my nest? Maybe two? I said yes. Then, sleeping on it, no. Irrational decision. Maybe not so irrational. A betrayal, but of what? At first I felt, "They're not my magpies. Take as many as you want." But after a while I started feeling like I didn't want to be responsible for another disturbance of the nest. Go find your own damn magpie.

Rain. Summer. The grasshoppers are hatching. Magdalena is not catching them with great agility. In fact, she isn't catching them at all. I did, however, catch her gumming a ladybug pupa (larva?). One of those crawling things on its way to becoming a ladybug.

The bird's-eye view. Like a camera, raising a bird changes the way you look at things. Intensifies and particularizes. Now when I herd sheep, I'm higher off the ground than usual. I see the sheep as if I'm looking *down* at them. Walking around with a bird on your head is like watching life from a tenement window.

A cricket in the house. I want to be the only one to have a magpie. All those childish, proprietorial feelings. Copy cat! Wanting to be special. Martha said she had a cricket and a spider for Magdalena (the spider was a black widow). Fierce, acquisitive motherhood.

Hannah will be be four tomorrow. Think how much she has learned in those four years, compared to what I have learned in the same time.

Magdalena does not get hungry at night. After dark, if I speak to her, she may open her eyes and look at me, but she will not beg. Like the chickens at roost. Completely out of it. What possible biological function could that nighttime coma serve? It serves coyotes, that's for sure.

June 7

Picnic in Cañon. Magdalena went to the river's edge, and I taught her how to drink in true passerine style, dipping water into the mouth (Goodwin, *Crows of the World,* thinks they suck it in too), then tilting the head back.

What did you see on this picnic? What did Magdalena see? A river of water, for one thing, shrunken from the flood to a clear stream. A reflection of oneself, man or bird. And did you say how Magdalena flew to the false man reflected in the studio window? Or how she got too deep in a pool of river water in the mountains, or how on the way home from town with your father, the cars were lined up at the flooded arroyo, all of them waiting to cross until someone else did first, to prove it was safe? Far from perturbed, everyone looked very happy in the face of trouble, this watery disruption of their lives. Everyone needs to have their life disrupted now and then. Something important always happens to us when the waters rise and recede. Noah and his gang. A starting over. Starting fresh. Jim Dekorne's aspen graffiti: "All beginnings are difficult." The rain always changes us. Talk of weather is not always idle talk. Storms are great events, and not only to country people.

Magdalena in her bath: "I know I'm supposed to be doing something with this water, but what?" Shakes her tail, plunges in. So that's what. The bathing virgin.

Magdalena, what is it in me that wants to have you all to myself? Others admire you, play with you. My objective voice says that you don't distinguish between one and the next, me and them. But how diligently I look for contrary evidence! Anything at all from you that will declare to the world, "This is my person. There is nobody else like him."

June 8
Magdalena's appetite seems to be falling off. Voracious up until now, going through fifty-pound sacks of dog food with a vengeance, cowing Pasco away from his bowl (not a cowardly dog, just good natured). But lately, she's been taking the food and spitting it back up, or tossing it away with a sideways toss of her head. Choosy? Cheeky? Wrong brand of dog food? Maybe birds just grow a lot all at once, until they can fly, then level off.

Other changes, too. Flight, for instance. At least, the rudiments of it. I gave her a new perch in the piñon in front of the studio. She slept there last night; this morning, she flew about seven feet from my hand to the tree. If it wasn't flying, it was one hell of a leap.

June 9
Hannah and I and Pasco, who couldn't be persuaded to go home, went to investigate the nest. Two adult birds scolded us, flew down over Pasco's head, but did not attack. Three young magpies in the branches near the nest, testing their wings. We could get very close to them, in spite of the parents' warning cries.

June 10
Morning. Summertime. Olympia's dogs got into the sheep again yesterday. I shouted them off, then they went after the young magpies, Magdalena's brothers and sisters, who have been taking short

flights from the nest along the riverbank. Fired one shot, and the dogs retreated across the river. To have denied the birds a human home, only to have them killed by dogs, who are here because of the people. Who can die a "natural" death any more?

Magdalena begins to roost out of my reach. Hannah asks, "Why do you want her to be alone?" Translation: on her own. I don't seem very convinced of any of the answers. Because she's a wild bird, and wild birds need to learn to take care of themselves, same as people.

Grandpa and Hannah arguing about the identity of potted plant. Grandpa: "You can't even *say* geranium." It was a pansy. Do we become children again in old age? What is it about the presence of parents that makes us feel something less than alive, when they're the ones responsible for bringing us here in the first place?

Dusk last night. A flock of magpies. One does not see a flock of magpies very often. Maybe a nesting brood, grown up but not yet mated, still the same old crowd. A shipment of cows, horses, sheep always sticks together, has an identity within and apart from the herd, even though they mingle with others. This consciousness of who they came with can last for years, manifests in small ways.

Magdalena is very interested in what I'm doing in this book.

What's the collective noun for magpies? How about "complaint"? There's a complaint of magpies in a cottonwood on the hillside across the river. The same ones I saw last night? Magdalena's siblings, fledged, exploring?

June 12

By the river, Magdalena on my shoulder. Suddenly she took off, flew across the water to the other side. I say "suddenly" because she had never done anything like that before, always stayed close. I didn't much like having the river between us. "Suddenly" because no amount of worldly wisdom can adequately prepare a parent for the child's leaving home. The real (what they call biological) parents arrived, scolding. Recognition? Were they telling her to come back home? Warning her to leave me before it was too late? Or just sounding a general alarm? Man in field. Hide your young.

I searched for her. For once, the faces of the young magpies all looked different, and I knew that if I had to, I could pick her out in a crowd. I also knew, from looking at those other faces, that she was what I had suspected her of being all along. Female.

She found me first. She returned, looming at eye level across the field, swooping up and down, and landed familiarly on my head. Not just any magpie. Mine.

June 13

Our hot days come in June. At work, Magdalena wilted in her cage, wings hung limply out from her body, mouth open, trying to keep cool. They are about to spray the whole county with grasshopper poison. If Sevin SLR doesn't kill birds, it certainly kills most of the above-ground insect population, which is what birds eat, which for my money is the same thing as killing birds.

Magdalena has been outside on her own for about a week, roosting in the piñon. Until now, food has been brought to her, but yesterday, she came to the food. Still no indication that she will learn to find her own, though. She'll lose herself in the leafage of raspberries and hollyhocks during the day, but who knows what goes on in there, play or work. At first sunlight each morning, she calls to me. It's not a sweet song. She saves all her sweetness for after breakfast, when, with a full crop, she'll stand on my desk, gaze at me with doglike love, whistle and chirp. Elaborations on the begging dance: she holds her wings away from her body, makes herself bigger (just in case I hadn't noticed the famished magpie jumping up and down in front of me). But only when very hungry. Her feathers have taken that iridescent, nacreous sheen you see on corvids and blackbirds. Her flight, still short and awkward, already has that characteristic magpie dip and climb.

Pica pica, Latin for magpie. At a writing conference, a poet friend made an unfavorable judgement on the English name for the bird, implying that the Tewa word was more beautiful and appropriate. "Magpie" quotes their temperament, if not their colors, movements, physique. They can be very unbeautiful creatures, especially when you live with one. God save the queen.

We have no cats here. Hannah and Molly in matching red terry-cloth robes. Elf One and Elf Two.

I'm clearing the riverbanks of dead willows, destroyed by some kind of scale, to give the sheep some new grass. The grasshoppers, like the willow scale, the beavers, the people — all pests — will come and go. Why can't they just leave things alone?

Actions and words. Shot the dog that killed my guinea hen. So it goes on. Dropped the dead guinea in the back of the pickup when

I took my dad to catch the plane back east, and chucked it in the arroyo across from the McCormick place. Hannah had fallen asleep, woke to say, "That's where we threw the rooster." I had forgotten, but to her, the event had already become part of the legend of her childhood. We had a mean rooster once. It used to spur her when she went in the barnyard, until one afternoon I got mad and kicked it over the fence. It lay there on the ground and didn't get up. Then its eyes turned to milk.

So that particular arroyo has become the graveyard of dead birds. What is this thing of mine with dead birds?

June 14
Magdalena pecked me in the eye this morning. Jealous, maybe, but jealous of what? The new cow? Magdalena no longer holds her position as the new beast. She's just another one of the old beasts now.

Too many animals: 1 cow, 1 calf, 2 goldfish, 6 big hens, 18 chicks, 2 guineas, 1 dog, 2 geese, 13 sheep, 1 girl, 1 magpie; 48 critters total.

Magdalena makes a career of complaining these days. Always clamoring for food. Making a nuisance of herself while I'm still in bed each morning. Old enough to be disciplined, but how do you discipline a magpie?

June 19
Late afternoon, Magdalena disappears. Maybe she was beginning to feel unwanted and returned to her own kind. Isn't that the way

all true-to-life wild animal stories are supposed to end? I realize that I have been neglecting her, not talking to her enough, letting her go hungry for long stretches to encourage her to hunt and make it on her own.

Now this. I've been walking around in a daze. Nothing squawks at me from the piñon tree each time I set foot out of the house. Dumb tree. I call to every magpie in the neighborhood, follow each flight, expecting her to appear out of thin air at any moment. No longer a pet, she'll become a regular visitor, I tell myself, a friend dropping in, surprising me when I'm milking the cow. One of the happy, uncaged spirits of the place. The lost child, raised by wolves, reclaimed by her own kind.

Near dark, I see a flock of magpies squabbling among the dead cottonwoods across the river. They are young. Their tails have grown to different lengths. From a distance, one looks familiar. I follow the flock, calling, but they are afraid of me. Their voices are different, too. I would know her voice if I heard it. Maybe. They don't know me, these magpies, they keep flying ahead when I get close. Could she have forgotten me so quickly? And what could have taken her away, unless the sound of a sister's voice?

I make believe I knew all along this would happen, but it doesn't work. I comfort Hannah, but it's more like she is comforting me. Magdalena has flown away to be with the other magpies, we tell one another, but neither of us believes it.

June 20
Hot days, the cotton flies out of the cottonwood trees. At San Juan,

it rolls across the hot asphalt, catches on rose bushes. No sign of Magdalena.

June 21

The grasshopper sprayers, two airplanes, came one day early. We had been told that if we didn't want our property sprayed we should hang white flags on the fence. Molly ran out with good bed linen, the first thing she could find.

The polemical art consists of having something to teach, but more often, an axe to grind. Do we invent our causes, just to have something to say? It's hard for the poor gringo to hate oppression, having never been oppressed, but we make a good show of it, hang our sheets on the barbed wire. The planes: mutant insects, grasshoppers that have survived chemical warfare and grown to monstrous proportions. The grasshoppers will be back, if not in such great numbers next year, the year after that. Next time, nothing will kill them.

June 22

She's here! She's alive!

In the early morning, I'd chased the flock of young magpies up the ridge. Was she among them? Does love come and go so easily? Then I ate breakfast and went to plastering the studio. I heard a familiar voice, as if in the distance, and then I heard it again. Ran back and forth across the yard in a tizzy. The call was in front of me, then behind. I had a sudden sick feeling when I realized it was coming out of the outhouse hole.

Dirty bird. Wallowing in it for almost two days, and never once, until this morning, did she cry for help. There she was, mired, looking up at me as if to say, "Well, what are you going to do about it?" A bucket on the end of a rope. Got her out, cleaned her up, set her back in her tree, and shoved some dogfood down her throat. Nothing quite as scrawny and pitiful as a wet magpie.

June 27
When she flies at me from a distance, with my whole attention focused on her, and hers on me, I fly too. It's magic to release a living creature from your hand into the air. Setting part of yourself free.

July 2
Magdalena torments all of us: Molly, milking; me, fencing; Hannah, all the time, hopping along the ground after her with that peculiar chucking sound, pecking at her heels. Sibling rivalry. When they fight, I threaten to drive out in the country somewhere and turn her loose. Idle threat. A neighbor came over yesterday in the middle of the ruckus. It's hard to make grownup conversation with a magpie standing on your head.

July 3
Stopped feeding Magdalena by hand. She's not a baby anymore. Instead, I'll leave a dish of dogfood out for her by the milking stanchion so she can eat whenever she wants. Between the new pup, Magdalena, and all the other magpies (word gets around, free eats), we really go through the Purina.

July 12

A vision. I came out of the house to let the cow out, and the air was full of magpies, laughing, one on every fencepost, one in every cube of sky. The world had gone mad with magpies. The magic that brought her here had gotten out of hand, like that favorite story of my childhood, the town (a town very much like La Madera) flooded with porridge when they can't remember the magic words. Stop, pot, stop! Only instead of porridge, this time it was magpies, as if to spite us with the inevitability of getting what we want. A magpie nightmare. A magpie siege. A plague of magpies. A magpie apocalypse.

Epilogue

There's not another word of Magdalena in the journal after July 3, 1981: "She's not a baby any more." That was the summer they didn't play major league baseball. She must have been killed sometime in August. In the middle of July, the journal entries start coming weeks instead of days apart, which means I had a job.

Sometimes she rode the dashboard with me to work. She got used to going places in the truck, the dump or the post office, and would come whenever she heard the door open, fly into the cab, and land on the steering wheel. The habit led to her early death: I went to get something out of the pickup one afternoon, slammed the door, and caught her in flight. She died instantly.

When it was just the two of us, she made a good companion, following me on walks in the hills or along the river. Sometimes I followed her. Flying ahead of me, weaving through the piñon forest where the other magpies nagged at us, she became a constant feature of my landscape, the artist's invariable signature. Other birds let me get closer with Magdalena riding on top of my head, or so I imagined, and the imagining made it so. As long as I felt alien to the natural life of the place, I would be just that; but by acting as if the other inhabitants had nothing to fear from me, even if it were just an act, I was allowed to approach. A native of the river junction — my ally, guide, relation — Magdalena admitted me to it in a way that I could never have entered all on my own. Occasionally, her companionship made me feel that I had as much right to be there as the grass.

At home, she got to be a terrible pest, divebombing the dogs; harrassing my daughter, a rival for parental affection; eating cherries off the cherry tree; preening people who preferred not to be preened; ruining the peace of our early mornings by scrabbling at the window panes and shrieking at us — Yeats's "miraculous strange bird." Towards the end, it seemed as if I were forever breaking up fights between the magpie and the other members of the family. If it hadn't ended as it did, I probably would have had the sad job of committing her to a distant, uncaring atmosphere.

Hannah and her cousin, Matthew, gave Magdalena a formal burial, in the local custom, planting a cross at the scene of the fatal automobile accident: "How but in custom and in ceremony are innocence and beauty born?"

Jangle Gently As You Move

Some kind of church doings, maybe. A baptism. But what were those men doing in the river by the bridge? Building something with rocks, it looked like. But in the middle of the river?

Cars and people. Ordinarily, in late June, on a warm, bright morning like this one, two or three cars at the most might park at the turnaround, local boys drinking beer and washing their cars. But it was the middle of the week, and there were cars everywhere, stacked up at the turnaround and lining the pavement all the way into town. People came on foot, too, as if on some kind of pilgrimage, the way they walked to Santuario on Good Friday. Grandmothers with babies, men in work clothes, kids (how careless they were! how unlearned in solemnity!). They crowded the far river bank and the guard rails on either side of the bridge, leaning over as far as they could go to get a better look. Some looked and walked back the way they had come. Others stayed, talked to neighbors. The river was about as far down as it was going to get, not even knee deep. The men hardly talked, passing rocks and shovelsful of sod from the riverbank to midstream. One of them wore a red bandana across his face.

I watched at the upstairs window. In the past, I had stood awake in the dark there, armed or unarmed, depending on how scared I was. But always in the dark, so they could not see me silhouetted in the upstairs window. It was at La Junta that I learned a reluctance to sit in front of an uncurtained window in a lighted room. It was like the Captain Video goggles we sent away for when we were kids, only the other way around: you can't see out, but they — whoever they might be — can see in. More than once I'd stood by that window, in the dark, with the Winchester on safe, trying to see what the bad boys, the banditos, the *hombres desesperados,* were up to at the turnaround. Other than the lit end of a cigarette, there was never anything much to see after dark, but I watched anyway. What would I do if they tried to steal my sheep or my firewood? What if they tried to get in the house?

The people came and went. Even before overhearing the conversation of the two women on the party line, I felt that whatever I was witnessing across the road would be with me for a long time and keep begging to be laid to rest. I knew the women from their voices, but it was hard to follow what they were saying. Something about a hand in the river. But whose? People always listened in on party line conversations, but without identifying themselves, as a way of letting the speakers know they needed to use the phone. A hand, that much was certain. But wasn't there anything more? Just a hand by itself, without a body? Two summers before, a rancher in Servilleta had found an arm wrapped up in a bale of hay. Or was it a finger? These things tended to change over the party line. So the news that someone had found a hand in the river was not without precedent. In stories that came by word of mouth from Spain and Mexico, the wicked bruja is forever getting decapitated or quartered but more often burned by those she has wronged. After the execution, they have a wedding.

Two squad cars arrived, and an ambulance, then Father Jerome, driving his new Volvo. He stood on the riverbank next to Jesús, the state patrolman, on the ridge of cobbles that the highway department had dredged up out of the river to keep it from jumping its banks in the spring, and read aloud from a book. The men stopped working and stood with bowed heads. Jesús was wearing a white surgical mask. I could see Father Jerome reading, but I couldn't hear what he was saying. A woman on the bridge started to cry, then to wail. They had to grab her, or she would have fallen. By the time Father Jerome finished his prayer, she was screaming bloody murder.

I remembered the boy then, missing for seven weeks. Could this woman be his mother? Her cry must have been heard clear into town at the post office, where the old men sat shaking their heads, and all the way up our little valley to La Zorra, scaring the dogs out of the shadows and making each of us stop what we were doing to listen.

"By now he's halfway to Mexico," said the stranger in the grocery store. He had been missing for three days then. Only a stranger would have had the license to say what everyone else was thinking, that he would not be seen again, alive or dead. He had too much to drink after the wedding that night, which, after all, is one of the things that weddings are for, to let people forget themselves, blow carbon out of their engines, raise their voices, laugh and cry and carry on in ways not ordinarily sanctioned. Weddings were remembered, in order from the least consequential to the most glorious, by how many people came, how much they drank, how many fights broke out, and who was left standing at daylight.

He had too much to drink and fell in the river, according to the most innocent version of what happened. But according to most people, he had had been beaten with the butt end of a rifle, and if not dead already, thrown unconscious into the river to drown. At any other time of year, he probably would have been found a few hundred yards downstream, washed up on the gravel or snagged by overhanging branches, his journey ended abruptly and unspectacularly. But when the river was up in April and May, pouring snowmelt out of the high meadows and picking up a heavy cargo of silt, along with anything else that got in its way — tires, timbers, a prolapsed cow, all the paltry and comical refuse of people — he would be taken far down the river.

Or so those of us who lived along the river liked to think. At least if he had been taken that far, he was out of our jurisdiction, and no further responsibility of ours. We would not have to carry him home when he got drunk, or bail him out of prison, or bury him. If he had not, as the president said of the seven killed in the space shuttle accident, broken the bonds of earth, at least he was firmly clamped into them, and in that sense, taken care of. His troubles had ended, but more than that, he wouldn't be any more trouble to us. He would not come looking for whomever had killed him. Pieces of him would not turn up in our haystacks.

People — mostly young men, even young men who had grown up together and were fond of one another when they were sober — always seemed to be killing one another in those hills. In the half dozen or so villages within easy travel of the river junction, if someone died, you were either related to the dead person or knew someone who was related to them. Never as remote as it seems in the cities, murder always had a name and a face: one led to another, and some of the feuds were so old that nobody, not even those who believed that they had been offended, could say who had thrown the first stone. Those who killed for the first time seldom went to jail, and those who went to jail had a way of showing up a few months later, all smiles. In the north, if you followed the thread far enough, everybody was related to everybody else, and the blood of kinship ran thicker than the water of the law.

Ramón, for example. He came to my door on a summer night, trying to escape from the brothers of the man he had just knifed. There was a baby in the house then, and I remember thinking don't let him in the house with the baby. He'd just "stuck" somebody, was the way he put it. He was still wearing the bloody knife on his belt. He didn't want to do it but he had to, he said. They'd forced him to it. Now they were coming to get him, and he needed to get away. He called me "bro" and asked if he could come in the house, or get a ride to La Petaca. I told him to hitch.

The brothers found him on the road nearby and beat him until he had just enough strength to get back and fall in a bloody heap on my doorstep. The police came and got him in the middle of the night. I found the knife in my yard the next morning, and gave it to Ramón's mother when she came looking for it. The wounded man died about a week later. They locked Ramón up for a while, but the case was settled without a public hearing. Not long after he got out, he was sitting in a pickup with three other men when someone opened up on them with an automatic weapon. Two of the four died. Ramón survived a head wound. He dropped by to see me one afternoon when he got out of the hospital, sober and in good spirits, a little heavier than before, grinning the way one who has repeatedly cheated death has a right to grin. He brought himself to my door like a prodigal son and said, as if there were any chance of forgetting, "Remember me?"

And Michael. Michael appeared in the hayfield late one morning. People did not ordinarily appear in the hayfield. They came by the road, in cars, on horses, on foot; or along the river, fishing; but never through the hayfield. There wasn't anything interesting in it, except to me. It wasn't on the way to anything. But there he was, slouching through my hayfield, worse for wear but with an unmistakable sense of purpose; like one of those mythic warriors, sprung from seed. He climbed through the fence and asked me who I was, something I wasn't used to being asked at home. But he thought nothing of asking it, and nothing of stretching the sheep wire all out of shape in the process of getting across the fence.

"Never mind who I am. Who are you?"

Michael, from Ojo Caliente. He explained that he had gotten beaten up and thrown in the river the night before (maybe getting thrown in the river had achieved ceremonial honors in the neighborhood, like getting your head shaved when you first cross the equator at sea), but that he had crawled out and slept on the river bank near my house, and that he was very hungry and could he please have something to eat. His clothes were wet and he showed me a fresh wound on his forearm. Maybe it was because Michael was so young (fourteen), but I felt a sudden and strong calling to make him a cheese sandwich. He took it without thanks, as if the only reason I had left the familiar and comfortable world of my upbringing and built a house by the river was to be there that morning when he materialized in the hayfield and feed him a cheese sandwich. I went back in the house for a minute. He was sitting at the picnic table devouring the food when I last saw him, and when I looked again, he was gone.

Michael, especially, I'm thinking of, because unlike the missing one, he had been in the river and returned, hungry and skinned up, but in full flesh, knowing something that he hadn't known before. Michael, because like all those who have entered the water and returned older, or humbler, or crazier; because he had whatever it took, if only dumb luck, to stay alive; what's more, to bring me the good news, to stumble across the hayfield and startle the sheep, tear up my fence, declare that the bad men had thrown him in the river but that he had come out in one piece, and that he was mighty hungry. That kind of news shouldn't be asked to go around by the gate.

They sent a helicopter out to search for the one who died after the wedding. It bombed up and down the Vallecitos all that week, scaring the calves, reminding us in our houses, doing the wash or writing our poems, of the one who had most recently gotten away; to say nothing of reminding us that in the flesh or in solution, we too would one day wash downstream, stopping on the way to fertilize somebody's corn patch, then on to the Gulf of Mexico. It came as a pleasant reminder, that helicopter. Each time it clattered off into the distance, upstream or down, the silence that came after seemed especially rich. Living in a quiet element, day after day, it was easy to forget about it: as easy as not hearing the river, being always immersed in its sound. It was a relief, too, to think that it could have been us instead of him, but that we had come through another winter and were there to see the corn come up again.

My daughter Hannah, almost five, was very interested in the helicopter. She wanted to know what was doing, and in the way adults have of making life seem happier and safer than it really is when speaking to children, wanting to put off as long as possible the knowledge of suffering and death when the simple, straightforward answer would not only satisfy curiosity, but also rout all the monsters that secrecy and deception give birth to, I told her not "what" they were looking for, but "who." As if, like Michael, he were going to return whole and happy from the flood.

"Maybe he drowned," she said, in the way that children have of saying exactly what's going on, instead of beating around the bush, like their parents. We walked down to the river one evening after supper. It had been raining. By the time we left the house, the water had gathered in the arroyos and heaped itself up in the riverbed, until the Servilleta that we found didn't look anything like its usual self. Except for a steady, chilling hiss, it didn't make much noise. Like water coming to a boil, it had gone quiet. When the river was high in the spring, you could usually hear rocks rolling along the bottom. The noise of the current stayed with you all day long, followed you into bed at night, and rose up out of your dreams to be with you first thing in the morning. But now, it had gone beyond all that uproar into a state of deep and terrible calm. The lower banks were gone. Where there had been land that very afternoon, the willows stood knee deep in water. At the corner of the pasture nearest La Junta, the river had taken in the fenceline. Partly drowned, the fenceposts looked helpless, as if they had started to do something and then forgotten what it was. The surface was unnaturally smooth, but turning. Great wheels of brown water swept past where we stood. It was a river we had never seen before.

Especially when out of control, water, fire, wind, and earth have a powerful effect on people. When I was a boy, a retired man in our apartment house belonged to something called the Fire Chasers' Club. His name was O'Reilly. When O'Reilly heard a fire engine — not just a loud fire engine, but any fire engine within even faint hearing — he grabbed his club blazer and ran or drove after it. Eventually I came to understand that O'Reilly and his club did not go to fires to help put them out or find out what had caused them or for any good reason, but just for the raw thrill of it. At the time, his behavior seemed neither odd nor childish. Who, given the opportunity to watch from a safe distance, wouldn't do the same? I certainly would have, if I'd been old enough. I longed to see the midnight sky ablaze, a lady in curlers leaping twelve stories into a stretched blanket. I think old man O'Reilly sensed that madness in me, saw a new generation of fire chasers rising out of the ashes of my protestant upbringing, for once he took me to his apartment to see his museum: an authentic-in-every-detail model of a hook-and-ladder (but no small, earnest firemen riding on it — why not?); framed photographs of famous fires, before, during, after; and best of all, a melted paperweight, which I was permitted to touch.

What is it that we love about disasters, especially the natural kind? As it is usually written, the history of nations is that of its wars; but the history of communities, and small ones in particular, recalls natural disasters: earthquakes, hurricanes, burnings, drownings. Like children, we ask again and again to be shown what we dread.

We walked the margin of the flooded banks to the bridge, where water stood in puddles. We didn't care. Our feet were already too wet from the grass to get any wetter. A tire came rolling down the river, not on its side, as you would expect, but standing up, riding the invisible axle of an invisible truck. And a baby doll without arms, refusing to drown. Entranced, we watched pieces of the world go by, things that had belonged to somebody, then gotten used up or thrown away, it seemed, expressly for our entertainment. We were glad to be high and mostly dry, witnessing but not touched by the deluge, and still in possession of all our arms and legs. We were glad not to have entered that gallery of broken baby dolls and drowned men. Pound as it would, the river could not reach us. The rain had stopped. The sun was coming back out, the way it does in this part of the world after a summer cloudburst. The road steamed.

"Maybe he drowned," she said.

Like the rest of us, she needed some kind of conclusion, and without waiting for evidence, reached the quickest and most obvious one. She insisted on watching when I butchered animals, even though it made her uneasy. She watched silently, faithfully, until the hide or the feathers had been taken off, the insides removed, then announced, with her delicate sense of rightness and ceremony, her need to call something by its right name, "Now it's meat, huh, Tom?" If the missing boy had drowned, becoming a what instead of a who, at least we knew what to call him. But lost, what was he?

It rained early in May, enough to make the young tomatoes and chilis lie down flat on the ground. We worried about them a lot more than we worried about the boy. It kept raining, and the Vallecitos, which should have been starting to slacken and clear, continued to rise. Most years, it fell to its lowest level by June, assuming its ordinary, unthreatening character. You could wade across then, and even if you got wet to your waist, there wasn't much danger of getting knocked down or swept away. But I like to remember the river in its darkest, most treacherous moods, the way it was that first week in May.

I was sick, and spent a lot of time looking at the rain out of the upstairs window. When the river was that high, it picked up whole trees, as well as the usual small-fry flotsam: branches, fenceposts, boards. Two concrete bulwarks supported the bridge in mid-stream. It happened that a tree had jammed between these bulwarks and began to trap other trees and branches, until the tangle threatened to send the river over its banks and take out the road. The men from the highway department came with a front loader, and for the best part of two days, tried to loosen the snags with a hook suspended by a chain from the loader's bucket. It was like that amusement park game where you try to make a Pepsi bottle stand up with a ring on the end of a fishing line, and just about as impossible. The men who worked for the highway department were dedicated and slow. It wouldn't do to hurry, one, because someone might think you you were trying to get ahead of them; and two, if you worked too hard you might finish what you were doing and find yourself out of work. With so much water coming down, there was no place to stand, no way to tie on to the snags except by lowering the hook, hoping it would catch on to something and break the jam. And if it didn't, you could always stand around a while, smoke a cigarette, drive the loader off the bridge so a car could cross, drive it back, watch the river go by, try again.

I ate aspirins and watched from my window as the rain came down. They could have dredged up the dead boy, if they'd let let their line go deeper. He may already have arrived by then, for all any of us knew, knitted into the tangle of uprooted brush and lost fishing lines. He could have been lying right there below us as we stood talking about him on the bridge that evening, buried except for the one hand raised like a judgement, waiting to be seen when the river went down. Maybe drowned. Maybe just pretending, making a joke on everybody. Maybe he'd taken off to Caleef for a little vacation and would be back in town next week with a suntan and new wheels, grinning at us like Death in his oxcart.

The highway men loosened the jam on the second day, saving us from a washout. I'd almost hoped they wouldn't. I wanted to find out what life would be like without a bridge, and my addiction to the goods and services that came from the other side. I guess I'd fallen in love with the idea of a washout. But no such luck. Before the bridge went in, some years before I moved to La Junta, there would have been no question of crossing the Vallecitos during the spring flood, especially not in a wagon or a car. So the river, especially the springtime river, made the people on one side different from the people on the other side by necessity, rather than by the usual things, prejudice or choice. The sense of this difference persisted after the bridge was built. At a slow walk, taking time to look at birds and stop on the bridge to look down into the water (and who, passing over water, can resist looking into it?), I would take about ten minutes to get from the middle of town (that is, the post office) to my place; and yet people who lived in town often asked how the weather was in La Zorra. A La Madera woman whose family had once owned my property said that she had always wanted to build a house there, exactly where I'd built mine; and would have, except for fear of the bad men who were said to rule that side of the river, who would ride down out of the hills as the Comanches had done within memory of the living, to steal and lay waste. So she had chosen to live in town (what she and others, even when speaking English, still referred to as the "pueblo," with its implications of mutual defense), safe from harm, surrounded by the loving attentions of friends and family. Who could blame her? I often longed for the same. To live on our side of the river, even though it was within sight of town and much closer to La Madera than the next cluster of houses on our side — La Zorra — was to live in enemy territory.

These are old fears. The ancestors of the people who now live in Santa Clara Pueblo, about an hour's drive south of La Madera, once lived in stone cliff dwellings and on top of the mesa at Puye ("the place where cottontails gather") to protect themselves from the raids of other tribes who habitually came down from the north — according to the literature distributed at the ruins — to steal "food and women." And when the United States government chose a site to build the bomb, it is no coincidence that they chose a mesa top naturally fortified by sheer cliffs — the same geologic formation that the cliff dwellers of Puye had burrowed into and climbed on top of a thousand years before.

I moved into the forbidden regions on the other side of the river without knowledge of the dangers, real or imagined. It was a beautiful place. I knew I wanted to live there for a long time, if not forever; at least until I became so thoroughly involved in its life that I would become just another one of its creatures; and until the place became such an integral part of me that even if I were driven from it or decided to leave on my own, I would already have learned it by heart, and so could never be entirely dispossessed. I wanted to watch the river go by and the seasons pass and not bother anybody. How could I have dreamed of enemies? On nights that I stood by the upstairs window, watching the firelight across the road and the figures that moved in front of it, figures that broke bottles, shot off guns, played loud music, and spoke words I could not understand, I had entered a tradition of fear — whether the fear of a child huddled in animal skins in a tufa cave at Puye, or that of a family in the eastern suburbs in the 1950s, deciding to install a fallout shelter instead of a swimming pool.

My rifle was a Winchester .30-.30, like the M-16, a weapon famous for the number of lives it had taken. A Cheyenne Indian once borrowed it from me to go deer hunting. Sitting in my living room, the butt of the rifle propped on his knee as if posing for a Curtis photograph, he commented, "If we'd had these, it would have been a different story." My father-in-law, a man with roots in the Ozarks who had moved to Texas and practiced law, gave it to me for a wedding present, the implication being that from then on, it was up to me to protect his daughter from savages of any color and all the ambushes that life would present; to order the wagons drawn in a circle and at the cost of my life, not allow her to be taken by another man. In the ten or so years I had owned it, I could remember firing it twice: once, trapped in a vegetarian commune and crazy for the taste of meat, when I killed and ate an old red rooster (being the toughest, stringiest old red rooster that ever lived, it was avenged); and again, to put a distempered cat out of its misery. But at night, when the bad men camped across the road and I stood by the window in the dark studying the unfamiliar substance of my fear, once or twice I had conceived of using it to protect home, livestock, family.

That May, after the boy was lost, and after his disappearance ceased to be a common topic of conversation in town, I took an afternoon to explore the Indian ruins in the hills above Ojo Caliente, a few miles below La Madera on the Vallecitos. Only what archaeologists call "housemounds" remained of the pueblo — a long, low ridge where adobe houses once stood. The mound took two turns and doubled back on itself, forming the plaza. It was a good place to look for arrowheads, especially after a rain, when they would be newly exposed and clean enough to catch the sunlight. I had been told by a collector that that was the best way to go about it, but I didn't care much for arrowheads. Finding them takes the same kind of devout and tireless patience that it takes to catch fish, or to go shopping at the mall on a weekend afternoon. I like Indian ruins for their silence, the sense of old time, and the reminders of mortality — not the artifacts. If I had been looking for arrowheads, I never would have found one; but as often happens when you stop looking or waiting for something, I was standing in the plaza thinking how nice that I didn't have to ruin the sleep of the place and the aimlessness of the afternoon by trying to acquire something (what I spend most of my time doing), when I looked down and saw one lying at my feet.

Amadeo Galvez rode by, looking for his lost white cow. I showed him the arrowhead, and he said that when they were kids they used to find them all the time — arrowheads, and bone needles, and the turquoise trade beads that turn up on ant hills. One time a rain washed away part of the arroyo bank, exposing a human skeleton. There were probably a lot more of them, too, he said. We were probably standing on graves that very moment without knowing it. Then he rode off, saying he'd appreciate it if I'd keep an eye out for a white cow without a calf.

The river was falling by June, the junegrass getting ready to turn red, the moon almost full, the wind blowing, the little bread-dough madonna smiling on the wall by my desk. Hannah, all pink, turned five. Pink barettes, pink nightie, pink cheeks. She opened her presents. A pink flamingo. A pink pig that walked and played the xylophone. We went to the swimming hole — not the little one at La Junta, "the bathtub," but the big one, miles upstream on the Vallecitos. I'd given people directions to this swimming hole, but wary of publicity, never very good directions. Cross the river. Drive until the road almost flattens out. You'll see some tire tracks leading off into the woods. Park under cover so they won't steal your tires. Walk down the hill. You'll hear the river in a couple of minutes. Follow it downstream until you think you've gone too far. You'll know the place when you see it. A steep, rocky canyon, where the sun goes down at two o'clock; a deep, green pool. Deep enough for a few lazy strokes, anyway, and plenty deep for a five-year-old just beginning to swim.

We rolled rocks into the gorge, delighted by the sound of big rocks entering water, the joy of letting things fall: all that action for so little effort. We dipped our hands in. Cold. I couldn't help thinking of the boy, wondering if he had passed through that very pool on his way to Mexico, which he must have, if he'd gotten that far; or if he might even be there yet, hugging the bottom; if he might reach out his dead hand, take hold of my living one, and say come with me. It was too cold to go swimming.

Junegrass, some call it. It ripens in June, when everything else has barely gotten started, turns red, but then, deeper than red, nearly purple. Some call it cheatgrass, because the animals won't eat it, or because it gets in the hay and when you buy hay with cheatgrass in it you get cheated. By early summer the junegrass had ripened and the cicadas started to carry on each morning. Satchel Paige had died. His rule number three for a happy life: "Keep the juices flowing by jangling around gently as you move." One after-noon, I could have sworn I heard a train whistle — the ghost of the old Denver and Rio Grande? The rooster cried "Alcohol!"

We had no more word of the boy. The community went about its business, though part of its life was being held hostage. No wonder that in stories, the unburied dead wander restlessly — an image that tries to console us for our restlessness, not theirs. State police cars went by right after he disappeared, or the same police car many times over, headed for that shrine of lawlessness, La Petaca. But not so much after that. Months might go by without seeing another. It was a long drive from Española, and dangerous to drive around asking questions in a neighborhood where police-men, forest rangers, livestock inspectors, tax assessors, and other foreigners were not always welcome. In La Petaca, they'd shot at the fire truck when it came to put out a fire.

We had no more word of him, and he entered the body of leg-end having to do with disappearances. In another nine hundred years, boys playing in the ruins of La Madera pueblo might chance on his remains, cemented into an old riverbed. Archaeologists would kneel and gently pull the earth away from his bones with their toothbrushes. European male, young adult, multiple skull fractures. Would they send for a priest then?

A fisherman had seen the hand sticking out of the riverbed that morning, and the word got around that there was nothing more, only a hand. But the rest of the body was there too, it turned out, and it would take some doing to get it out.

He had been gone seven weeks. I had already imagined what a body looked like after seven weeks in the the water, so what kept me from looking, like everybody else? How much worse could the real thing be? He had traveled ten miles as the road goes, more in river miles. Had he come all at once, in the night, in the dark rush of springtime waters, or had he taken his time, turned in the eddies, paused on the upstream side of rocks until the current took him back? But what puzzled me most, and what I still wonder about now and then, is what stopped him precisely there, by the bridge, the only place within miles upstream or down where it was almost certain, when the water fell, that he would be found? He could just as easily have stopped under the bridge north of town, where people hardly ever walk, and where he probably would have stayed until he dissolved completely. Maybe he wanted to do something right for a change, even if it was dying. There at La Junta, women cried for him who never would have cried for him had he lived. The priest drove all the way across the hills from El Rito to stand on the riverbank and read a prayer, even though the smell must have been overpowering, and even though the boy had been anything but a good one. Why else would he have come to rest where people walk almost every day, where fishermen from Texas park their cars to make a few casts; where the bad boys, his compadres, come to drink because nobody bothers them there; where Mr. Ortega, the town patriarch, drove each morning to pick up the aluminum cans from the night before because he could sell them, but also because it was his duty to know everything that went on in the community, and that is where the community ends; where I had walked a hundred times, seeking solitude, and the companionship of elementary things, rocks and water; in short, the only place it was absolutely certain that somebody would find him.

He was planted in midstream, almost entirely buried in sand. They had to dig him up so they could bury him again, and they were building a dam to keep what little was left of the river off to one side. They couldn't just leave him there, cover him up with some rocks and have done with it. No, of course not. That would have been against the law.

PERILS NOT INSURED AGAINST

On August 1, 1747, attacking Indians stole twenty-three women and children from the village of Ojo Caliente, a few miles downstream from what is now La Madera. I wonder if life here is much safer now than then. Ojo is still isolated, unincorporated, lacking the safety of numbers or municipal law enforcement, although last year the area finally got its own state patrolman. The volunteer fire department put out a grass fire once, and they still talk about it on bingo nights when money is raised to keep the engine gassed and repaired. Last winter the Head Start bus (really a car) hit a patch of ice, slid off the road, and landed upside down in a ditch. If my daughter or any of the other four children on board had needed to go to the hospital, an ambulance would have had to come thirty-five miles one way — too far to sustain any serious belief in outside help. No bugle will sound. No pony soldiers will appear on the rim of the mesa. And I notice that my homeowner's insurance does not cover me for "hostile or warlike action by any government or sovereign power, *de jure* or *de facto*."

Ojo Caliente came up short again last fall. We needed a certain number of three- and four-year-olds to qualify for our own Head Start program, and as in years past, we just didn't have them. Then something political happened and the quota was met — or ignored. The word went out that if parents were willing to pitch in and fix up a room in Ojo's old school building, we would have school after all.

The school building stands across the river from "The World

Famous Ojo Caliente Hot Mineral Springs," our quaint, moldering resort and spa. For $4.15 you can sweat off your hangover, or whatever else ails you. Amarillo businessmen come to parboil themselves in the pool and drink the medicinal waters: arsenic for digestive troubles, lithia for madness. Nearby, pigeons coo in the bell tower of a disintegrating sod and adobe church where early settlers sought refuge from Comanches and Utes. They were nomads, opportunists, dealers in children as in livestock or any other tradeable commodity, remembered still in the threats of mothers to their kids. "Behave, or I'll sell you to the Comanches."

The room had not been used for years. Bubbling plywood shut out the sun and protected a few but not all of the windows from the rocks of vandals. There was a mildewy, institutional smell, one that I have finally placed: the recreation hall at Incarnation Camp, Ivoryton, Connecticut, where rowboats and mattresses were stored over the winter. Mostly mothers, but also a few dour fathers, myself included, patched, painted, scrubbed, and carpeted. Even after school started it took a while for the scent of decay and uselessness to wear off. True, it was brighter than before, and the walls were getting filled up with the sure signs of education — lists of names and doings, gummed metallic stars awarded for skill or sleep, coon-faced dogs and spidery suns, houses with smoke coming out of them, this one a secure house, that one about to be launched from its foundations. But things didn't really come to life until the two gerbils arrived, a contribution of the teacher's boyfriend.

Gerbil: any of various old world burrowing leaping desert rodents. Everybody gave it the hard *g,* as in "Gerber's," and by the time one of the parents called them "jerbils" it was too late. We already knew how to say it.

Gerbils were just what the school needed. Unlike the children, they would not go away at night to another, better place. They could be relied on to be there every day, fully alive and at home, getting nowhere on their treadmill, juggling pieces of bread feverishly in their little hands. But other things were needed as well. Cages built around the gas heaters so the kids wouldn't get burned. There was a sort of playground: bare dirt, tumbleweeds piling up against a cyclone fence, hazards of all kinds to be cleared away before children could even go there, much less play. The treasurer of the parents' committee said we had a little money left over from the bake sale, not enough to do anything with, though. Resolved: we would sell tickets to a Sunday pancake breakfast and raise enough for a swing set. We would have the sale right across the hall from Head Start in the Senior Citizens' Center and catch all the hungry people on their way home from church.

The pancake breakfast was a mild success. Bands of the public spirited stood in line, got their pancakes, scrambled eggs, coffee, and orange juice, and sat dutifully at the one big table that was really many gin rummy tables put together. They ate without much talk or apparent hunger, wishing they were home and it was enchiladas. Someone had picked a few dry weeds out of what was to become the playground and put them in a vase on the table to remind us why we were there. By the time it was over, we had cleared $170 — enough to order a swing set out of the Sears mail order catalogue. Maybe it wouldn't be top of the line, but it would do.

Meanwhile, as if to mock our perennial shortcomings as parents, the gerbils increased from two to seven. Even before the babies were weaned the teacher started to campaign for their adoption. Gerbils were easy to take care of, she insisted. They could live in a shoebox and eat eggshells. In fact, they *liked* eggshells.

We had too many critters at home as it was, so I never considered the possibility of a gerbil until Hannah approached one morning and asked me to write out the words "Hannah wants a baby mouse" on a piece of paper. If she had asked permission to do what she was trying to do, I would have said no. But there was such tight-lipped, passionate determination in her, such lively contempt for household bureaucracy, that I didn't. I substituted "gerbil" for "mouse" and handed the paper back to her. Not a word of thanks. She ran downstairs and typed it over. That way it would look more official. More parental.

Peanuts arrived that same afternoon — not a baby at all, it turned out, but a full-grown procreating adult male. The father. He moved immediately into a rusty birdcage where he would stay visible and within the bounds of our love. Where had that old birdcage come from? Kingdom of gorging ravens, the La Madera dump? I couldn't remember. I did remember its last captive, though — a pet magpie, crushed at last in a slamming door and buried with full pomp by Hannah's city cousin. A ring of wildflowers, bits of pretty stone, two juniper sticks tied together for a cross. Around here, we live with the expectancy of sudden loss.

I tried to impress this on her. Small animals must not be squeezed, I said, not lifted by the tail the way they did at school, not allowed to run loose where they might get stepped on or caught in a mousetrap or eaten by Franklin, the cat. Sometimes you might not even mean to hurt something and it might get hurt anyway, I told her. Accidents can happen. Do.

La Clinica del Norte, our debt-ridden outpost of modern medicine, is a short drive across the hills in the town of El Rito.

Hannah was feeling better on our way over that morning. A gray morning. We were both supposed to be other places. Her finger, wrapped in a bloody paper towel, had stopped hurting so bad, and she pointed out things of interest along the way. A cave. A newborn calf.

She remembered the last time she had been to the clinic, the morning the Head Start bus went off the road. The crying children, the broken glass. "James had a crash car," was the way she had first tried to explain it. "The car went backwards," meaning it had turned upside down. She told us about the car's engine, oddly visible in that position. No one had ever told her cars could do that. It was hard for her to talk about it at first, but then it came all at once, a flood of description. People she knew who had died or been hurt got mixed up in the story, her grandmother, and a friend of the family who had been in a bad car accident. Then anger at the driver, James, "for treating us bad that way." James came by later to see how she was doing, told how he had found the children in a pile in the back of the car with Robert Montoya on the bottom, the little boy from Petaca who couldn't speak any English when he first came to school, but who wouldn't stop talking in the doctor's office. "Hey, man, you should of seen it. The car turned over, man. We were in it."

At the clinic her records were taken out of the file, and for the first time I saw the official account of injuries. Bump on head. The doctor was a friendly, solicitous young man who wore no white coat. He soaked the finger in a soapy red solution and explained the dangers of infection. He'd never heard of a rabid gerbil, but just to be on the safe side, he wanted to call the communicable disease people. While he was on the phone we waited quietly and stared at a medical chart on the wall. It was the lateral cross section of a child — child on the half shell. "You could see everything, huh?" said Hannah.

The doctor returned, smiling. There was nothing to worry about. Gerbils were not known to carry rabies. He also observed that, pathogenically speaking, the bite of a man was far more dangerous than that of any animal.

She was bitten three times before we had to send Peanuts to the penitentiary, Hannah's cousin in the city. Her devotion was fierce, but the gerbil was fiercer. Head Start has yet to order its swing set, and even when we do, there'll be a wait. Sears does not like to come this far because it's not on the way to anything. The other Saturday a few parents braved the wind to plant truck tires on edge in the playground (as if it's not hard enough to get a head start in life, we've given them an obstacle course). I paid off my insurance, for all the good it does me. We're alive and well in Ojo, preparing for the next attack.

GIFTS AND CREATURES

April 5

Eudora lambed this morning, both pintos, like her. The goose sits strong on her nest, the gander doesn't seem to know what to do with himself. A nest is one place out of all possible places, not the best place or the worst place, but one place, and it will do. Once she begins to sit, there is no longer any question of choice. Like the sign over the front door of a trailer home in Chamita: "We are satisfied." But what do you do with the yearning to go someplace else for a change? Merton, on a rare occasion, leaving the monastery to do business in town, and discovering that he didn't miss it after all. But isn't there a certain kind of salvation in getting away and seeing new things, the face of a woman passing on the street in Louisville? The lucky ones don't have to leave the monastery to see new things, but for the rest of us, sometimes, doesn't it help?

April 6

Cutting latillas in the mountains. Every so often something falls away and I see this country again as a foreign land, it shines the way it might shine in my imagination if I ever left here, or had never been. The thing is to get to the edge, where nothing has been determined, nothing seen, and you don't know what's going to happen next.

April 7

Spring fever, 102 degrees. A pair of owls on the river last night, and just the one this morning, up with a sick child. I like owls. I like their calls and the soundlessness of their flight. Just a trace of a superstition lingers. More than once, embarking on a course of action and seeing the owl, I could have turned back, but didn't. Each time, something painful happened, but when have there been times without pain?

A circumstance, an event, a place: even if we have to leave, we keep coming back until we come to some kind of an understanding.

Wind, cloud. In the outhouse last night, I watched flimsy clouds brush against the moon. They were pink clouds, and the ones over there to the south were heavy, but white. I thought: wouldn't it be nice to save that? And the white dog in the blue night, barking at his echo.

April 8

Dog attack 5:15 a.m. All survived. A story of a man who shoots the neighbor's dog. The story addresses a mystery, but does not solve it. It speaks of a longing in us, but witnessed in the longing of someone else. Whatever it is that I want must be very close, not far away and hard to get to. It takes a leaping, maybe. Surgery? The ability to walk through walls? I know it's right here but sometimes I feel like I have to get away to see it, but then it won't be here any-more, but there. So why leave?

Molly's papier-mâché coyote head in living room, to be worn in a parade in Santa Fe. She slept on the couch all night long, never even took off her shoes. When I really allow myself to listen to her, instead of opposing her — the usual thing — she is a great teacher to me. She's restless. She wants to be one of those people who've done things.

Ad in *Thrifty Nickle:* "CASELDA, whatever happens or can happen, has already happened before. God makes the same thing happen again and again. Everything that happens in this world, happens at the time God chooses. I love you, Caselda. Love, your husband, Bumper."

Tin can rolling down the road, very sure of itself, very businesslike.

Easter morning
He is risen, He is not here. But Easter's a lot older than the death and resurrection of Christ. It's in the rocks. Hannah sings:

> *Jelly bean, jelly bean, jelly all the way,*
> *How what fun it is to ride in an open riding sleigh.*

In the park, two slinky girls from Texas in a dying VW bug dump off a fat derelict. Softball game, the cover coming off the ball, until a graceful young man in clean white baseball shirt and clean white shorts and a curly girl, the two fresh from love and bath, come into the game with two brand new white softballs. I was leaning on the chinup bar, some kid asked me to move over, grandpa, so he could use it.

That song has been going through my head: "There was something in the air that night, the stars were bright, Fernando." Hannah in her pink Easter dress, "Mom ironed it so it's not crip-

[177]

pled." For grownups, the difficulty is not in finding the right word, but in avoiding it.

April 12
The day after Easter. Terrible Easter. We fought about money. What are we really fighting about?

April 15
Why is it that when I go away from here, everything seems so interesting? Two old San Juan women, sisters, examining the rotted cactuses in the produce department in Safeway. Cheyenne-looking man with a red cloth tied around his head, kneeling by the highway, working the knot of a plastic sack full of beer cans, very serious about it, like rolling a prayer smoke. Man who has just caught a ride and is running to the car, that look of triumph on his face, the joy of a man who has just caught a ride after a long wait.

Ditch day. In Spanish you don't "clean" the ditch, you "take it out." Its different parts have different moods, different resident spirits, and as you work up, you say hello, remember them from all the other ditch days, the easy-going spirits and the demanding ones, the place where the hill comes down every winter and must be taken out again every spring. If you don't clean the ditch, it will disappear, become nothing more than a weedy, snaking mound at the foot of the mountain. The water will stay in the river, where it wants to be, and never reach the fields. We wouldn't have "all these good things," as Tony calls them: grass, alfalfa, cattle, money, food, life. But we also wouldn't have to clean the ditch.

April 16

The terror of going back to work. The falling out of oneself, like falling out of a window.

I call Molly "Molly," rather than "my wife," when speaking or writing to someone who doesn't know who she is or what she is to me. Who can say what one person is to another? My this or that.

April 17

The table, cleared, invites more things to be put on it. So why clean house?

April 18

Smell of water in the fields. The killdeers don't bother to come around until there's water in the fields. It's still blowing. In the garden, the straw mulch has all blown away in the wind. His great work completed, St. Thomas said that the *Summa Theologica* was "all straw."

The goose has been setting for almost three weeks now. Her life has ceased. She is melting into the world. Her orange parts — feet, beak, eye rings — are hidden. She sleeps with her head tucked under one wing. The dog doesn't see her when he trots by: she stirs and hisses, returns to this world for a moment, then sinks back in. Thomas Merton writes, "An animal cannot be a contemplative." He has not seen my setting goose. Sometimes I think it's a lot harder to strike a balance between the contemplative life and the life of commerce than it is to do either one exclusively. When you try to do both, you do them both half-assed.

Morning. The sun, at the end of its winter migration, comes up in the bowl between the two hills. The crows cry "Java! Java!"

April 20

I want to be dark; I am pale. When I was a boy I used to take an aluminum lawn chair up on the roof of 83 Park Terrace West and try to get a tan. I imagined I was a dark man making love to a girl I was in love with. Once she did a split on the beach and I could see a few dark hairs down there, which made me wonder, because she was fair like me. One of my friends in grade school was Theodore, one of very few black kids at P.S. 98. We used to walk home together for lunch, and sometimes we'd eat a bag lunch on a bench in the park. He'd had polio when he was a baby so he walked with a deep limp, as if he were reaching down to pick something off the pavement with every other step. Instead of running, he skipped — the one bad leg, his luggage, dragging behind. When we played punchball in the schoolyard, Theodore hit what should have been a double and got thrown out at first base, but he always laughed, even when he got thrown out. He came to me in a dream last night. I told him I was writing stories and he said, "Give it up. The truth is better than anything you could ever invent."

April 21

The television's still broken, so I didn't get the Falklands news until I went to the store to get a loaf of bread. Manuel Griego said the English submarines were coming. His eyes were like two sacs of water: the look of them was down under and behind. He will be ninety in December, the only Republican in town and one of very few Protestants. His wife died not long ago, and one day in the post office he told me, "I'm not making any plans. I just live from day to day." Mr. Griego likes to talk politics. I apologized for my television and not knowing what was happening in the world. The British fleet is on its way. Our president is taking a conciliatory line, but the queen is outraged. The queen is extremely upset. Cristina writes up our loaves of bread. Manuel Griego looks at me from his place back there, down under the water, and explains the situation. His eyes widen and fill as he speaks, but my mind wanders. I am back at work, pushing over the outhouse. Nobody had used it for years. At first I thought I couldn't push it over by myself but then it lost its balance and fell quietly with a sort of wooden sigh, relieved from the trouble of standing upright and being useless. There was nothing under it but a rat's nest and a few toys: Frankenstein in a Jack Dempsey crouch, a couple of army tanks, and a Spanish galleon — the plastic kind that comes in a kit and you glue it together following instructions. Two tiny soldiers stood on deck. They were still glued there even though someone had thrown them down the outhouse hole and the rat had buried them under his stash of corncobs and gum wrappers and a teething ring. One sailor faced port and the other starboard, but otherwise they were the same: left hand welded into the hip, the right extended, reaching forward as if to shoot someone or shake hands. ". . . and the English government has done nothing to educate the people or improve their way of life." Manuel Griego's eyes were like oceans. Small armadas were setting sail in his eyes.

April 22
Molly's getting ready to leave for a show in Dallas. Her open suit-

case on the couch, portfolio, sweatshirt, a biography of some artist. The cat watches the bird. Desire plays like a flame in his eyes. He is trying hard to forget or to pretend that he doesn't care, but he can't do either thing.

At work, the two old men came out of the house to see how things were going. Old man Trujillo complained about Reagan and people on food stamps, said you couldn't get anyone to buck hay anymore. Old man Mauro shows me where the wind moved a fencepost. Some kind of wind to do that. His weeding shovel is worn down to a sickle moon. Sometimes he sits outside in the shade of an almost-dead apple tree. It hardly has any leaves, but he does not belittle the shade. He takes what there is and imagines the rest of it. People get less critical with age, especially when we see how little we have accomplished, how good those few, shriveled, wormy pieces of fruit are.

Asparagus in snow. Asparagus is a strange plant with a strange name. Look at it for a while. It looks like a plant someone made up, something that would grow somewhere else, anywhere but here. It grows with unnatural speed, like a time-lapse movie. Don't turn your back or it will go to seed. Asparagus . . . who would think it? God makes a joke. Asparagus might grow in the landscapes of psychedelic artists, or be a tree in Dr. Seuss. It has scales, like certain reptiles. It quickly becomes erect. It makes me vaguely uncomfortable to know there are asparaguses growing in my garden. Beware the Asparagi. They will come and impregnate your daughters in the night.

The dishes always look so pleased to be washed.

April 24

The slab is poured. The frozen chops are in the sink, and Hannah whimpers at the end of her dream. Steam from the croup kettle. Petey the finch picks at his sandpaper. I woke in the night worrying about Clorinda's shed, which I have been working on. Yesterday she said if it blows away, she will get me; and if it blows away after she is dead, she will haunt me from the grave. I will hear things in the night and know it is Clorinda, come to trouble me about her shed that was not built to stay put the way I said it would.

April 25

Ulceration of the spirit. It seems that when I have a job, my life becomes the job and not much else. There is no true rest and no true work until it's over. Drove to town (again) in a frenzy (again) to exchange some items, make right what I had convinced myself was wrong. And what of the frost, the clear morning, the pregnant sheep, this desk?

William Goyen on place [*In a Farther Country*]: "You must first desire to live within your own heart."

April 29

A surfboard on top of a car, so far from the surf. I know there was something else, many other things that need to be rescued from the oblivion of a working day. There were three new lambs in the morning, but they no longer seem especially remarkable. There was something else I saw or noticed that I wanted to write down. Yes. An orange steamroller in Española.

Life without television. If you get stuck teaching English in a small redneck town, you can always write a small redneck novel.

April 30
Old man Mauro is 96, and his boy doesn't want him to have a garden. I say let him have a garden. A big one. More than he can handle. Let him die at the end of his sickle-shaped shovel. Isn't it better to die in your garden than in some hospital? It's better not to die.

Senior: I've got to plant my melons. If you go to town, get me some seed, will you?
Junior: I'm not going to town.
Senior: (hobbling back to the house) All right. I'll leave you alone.

He told me a story. This was back in Italy, I suppose. Once, unloading a boxcar full of macaroni, he unloaded more than he was supposed to. He unloaded a whole boxcar full of macaroni by himself and got fired for it. The big boss heard about it, kept Tony on, and fired the foreman.

Clorinda: "If any *ratones* get into that shed, I'm going to give you hell."

May 1
Do I want to teach in a community college in Thatcher, Arizona? Molly: maybe one in a thousand will show some kind of a spark. There may be a way out of it, ask for more money than they're willing to pay. We may be dreaming. There may be nothing, no future, no life after La Madera. Now we have become the young

folks out on the farm, yearning for those city lights.

May 3
Linda, Molly's art teacher, reminded me that these days, in cultured female company, you do not make any general statements about females. I'd ventured that Death was a woman.

May 4
Old man Mauro's got a deck of cards so old they're worn down to cameos. In the old country, he says, when it's dry and doesn't rain, they say someone hasn't been going to church. On the last day of the job, he walked out to where I was working, putting the door on Clorinda's new shed. He told again of the great wind that had come and blown away the old shed. He showed me his stash of old railroad ties, taken from the abandoned spur of the Denver and Rio Grande that ran to La Madera from 1914 to 1927. "We got lotsa wood," says Tony. I was in a fit to get done, didn't have time. "Looks like I might never get out of here," I said, to let him know I couldn't stop this time, couldn't listen. "Oh yeah," he said, and walked away. At 96, not much chance of his getting out of there either.

Why do I always have to be rushing headlong into the next thing? Why can't I just be where I am?

May 6
Molly: in her family, it was nice for a girl to have talents, especially artistic talents, and to practice them apart from the serious business of making a living. For a woman, work, effort, creation, were merely ornamental; they didn't have anything to do with survival.

[185]

If you wanted to survive, you got yourself a man to provide for you. One of the ways of getting a man was to have talents. In my family, literature was something to be appreciated, not made. The real business of life, especially for a boy, was to get a good education and a good job, maybe teaching or something of the kind that would allow you to continue expressing your appreciation. Then you could go home at night and read until in your exhaustion the book fell over your face.

Walter Abish: "When something becomes terribly familiar we stop seeing it." Does this mean I'll have to leave La Madera, be in another place and time, before I can find out what's happening here, come to know the people living in this house?

May 8
Sick for days, and still weak. Boy in the supermarket bouncing a tennis ball off his sister's head. She had the kind of beauty that does not yet suffer for having an older brother bounce a tennis ball off her head. On the railroad tracks yesterday morning, feeling the way you do when you walk along railroad tracks. Slim, cigarette-smoking switchman, cowboy hat. Home to La Madera, my play-dough virgin sitting on the desk, my wall, my corner of the bed-room. Sometimes I feel like we're already moving away from here, that it's something that has already been undertaken in our hearts although we have not yet said that it will happen. But where would we go? What would happen to all the animals?

May 10
Molly's journal entry: "Tomatoes froze. Slept all day. No lambs."

May 11

I am a construction worker. Today I put on my Charlie-construction-worker boots. One day soon, I will put them on no more.

Phyllis McGinley, *Lives of the Saints:* "The trouble with most of us is that our souls are not strong enough to survive the corroding effect of daily living."

May 15

Yesterday a man came and talked to me across the wall. He said he knew everything. Now I'm kicking myself for not asking him a few questions.

Just now, a meadowlark. Can't remember hearing one here before, the hills are too close, and they like open places. I'm still hung up on birds. In Jung, the bird is transcendence. I can't transcend transcendence. Also, a painting by a person "undergoing therapy": one half red, "body," a howling wolf; the other half blue, "soul," an angel. And at the meeting place of body and soul, a "mandala-like" green plant. Like the peyote shawl, half red, half blue, and the green plant reconciling the two. Willem de Kooning: "Forms ought to have the emotion of a concrete experience. For instance, I am very happy to see that grass is green. At one time, it was very daring to make a figure red or blue — I think now that it is just as daring to make it flesh-colored." Whenever I hear a meadowlark, I'm back in Visalia, California, where the Dodgers have a farm club.

"I've taught everything," said the man across the wall. "Vocational, academic. I know everything." He'd also been a justice of the peace and needed a shave badly.

May 19
Anything might happen. We might sell the house. I might get a job. Someone might give me some money, recognize sleeping genius, sponsor my life. Someone might let me do what I want to do. I might let me do what I want to do.

May 20
Went walking in the mountains. Far below and away, the Duke City teepee burner. The world not as towns and roads but as mesas and valleys and rivers. Get up and away a little bit and man's work disappears, all except his smoke, his smoke.

May 21
Saw a boy beating up a mailbox, a girl in purple pants carrying a bouquet of purple flowers.

May 22
From *Scott's Last Expedition*:

"I am inclined to see much favor of tea."

"One is much struck by the importance of realizing limits."

"The sun has been shining all night."

"It is very difficult to say if we are going up hill or down."

"Things beginning to look a little serious."

May 23
Hannah saw a rooster get on a hen: "Why do they do that?" "That's how they make little chickens." "You and mom do that. She gets on your back."

My work's gone to hell, where it usually goes when I've got a job. But as they say, *un buen gallo canta en cualquier gallinero.* A good rooster sings in any chickenhouse.

May 26
The river's on its way down. In a little more than a month, Molly's off to art school in Tennessee. The less we see of each other, the more we seem to respect each other.

May 27
William Gass: "Of course there is enough to stir our wonder anywhere; there's enough to love, anywhere, if one is strong enough, if one is diligent enough, if one is perceptive, patient, kind enough — whatever it takes."

June 6
Dear Diary,
    We have an offer for our home and the man who's making it didn't even look at the bathroom. The place wasn't even for sale but he heard from the realtor that we might be interested in selling. He looked around for about ten minutes and said "I'll take it," and all we could think to say was that it wasn't for sale, not now,

anyway, maybe never. Maybe he doesn't know there's no toilet. I feel like the ignorant dirt farmer who can't believe there's as much money in the world as what this man is offering, my barefoot children taking refuge from the stranger behind my long, shadowy legs, my woman drying her hands with a potato sack on the porch, keeping out of it. How have you been? Sometimes when I'm working more than I ought to be I see something — the man walking his two scottish terriers on a leash during his lunch break — and I think of you, but at a distance, the way I might think of my dead mother or my family living far away, and I wish I could live closer to you, write in you more often than I'm able.

In El Rito yesterday I drove with my five-year-old daughter (new yellow party dress, but dark and unshod feet) to send a story to a man in Missouri who might offer me a job. And what then? Moist, tragic young women writing stories about the beach, believing everything I say even though I don't believe it myself?

June 10
The white hen in the cool dark alley at Giron's, sunlight down at the other end.

June 11
Coming out of the country, things we might have done we are not doing. Molly's fixing a gate for the coyote fence, but does it really matter how it hangs if we're not here to use it?

Found this calendar in an old journal, when things and we were different:

Feb 12   Moon waxing, pisces (root development)

Mar 15	Castrate kids
Mar 19	Molly's period [with a star]
Apr 8	Butcher kids. Plow cornfield. Plant potatoes. Rain at night.
Apr 13	Found aphids and ladybugs on roses.
Aug 1	First ripe tomato.
Oct 7	Ecolet broken [my handwriting]
Oct 8	Ecolet fixed [Molly's]
Oct 14	Rabbits due; no rabbits
Dec 9	– 19 degrees F. in the morning. Molly says, "I don't think Beethoven's all that great."

Now we do things halfway. Even sleeping and eating we do as if giving in to them, being defeated by them.

Sitting here this afternoon, I could have sworn I heard a train whistle. The ghost of the Denver and Rio Grande? Dead cat across the road. All dead things smell the same. The cicadas started up at nine this morning, yesterday was the first I'd heard them. Not listening, likely. Yates's cow aborted, his sheep bloated. In Los Alamos, Mona gave a lecture on her turkey blanket, and best in show went to a mastadon-ivory horse. At the end of round nine, Cooney was getting whipped. We lost our reception past Medanales. The flies have come. Flies and cicadas.

Looking for the place in Molly's dream, the place we're supposed to live. Chimayo, Santuario, La Puebla, Santa Cruz. Crossed the river, woman in Volvo following. The boy fishing, the mother waiting, arms folded. I waved to the boy, who looked drugged or somehow not quite there. Woman in Volvo drove through ditch that I thought we should not drive through. Decided to turn around and go back. Boy holding eight-inch fish with battered head. He still would not smile. Across bridge, lovely green lane, white and pink sands, Russian olive. Is this it? No, not here, I'll know it when I see it.

Hannah calls the atlas "the going places book." If we didn't know the language, what languages we would know!

The man who wants to buy the place lives in Hollywood, California. Name's Newt. Got a written offer from him yesterday.

June 21
Is the small red eye in the egg really a chicken? This is the day by which we must sell our house or not sell. The cat eats anyway. He does not know that the house might be sold away from him. He eats as usual, and licking, casts a bitter look at the bird. In California, Newt turns spotless eggs. We won't sell. Not yet, anyway.

June 26
Márquez: "He had loved her so much and for so long that he could no longer conceive of any suffering that did not begin with his wife."

A bird I don't know, a sad trill, nothing too energetic, a run of notes, monotone, resigned.

Marriage is a commitment beyond us, the giving up of oneself. We say we will do what it is impossible to do, know what it is impossible to know, that we will love this person no matter what comes. Under those conditions, only God should marry.

June 29

Tierra blanca. No rain today. The blue blanket over the French doors, our air conditioning. Agee on Dreiser: like a bad translation of a Russian novel. But he finds something "excellent" in that clumsiness, something you can't account for by grammar or grace. Grace in its redemptive sense: the meaning comes through and reaches people in spite of themselves, something beautiful and good beyond our ability to say what makes it beautiful and good. It comes when we don't expect it. It is the thing we can't "accomplish."

That English becomes a "conceptual" language and Spanish an "emotional" one, as some say, is the fault of its practitioners, not the language. The language serves our dearest wishes. If we want to get rich, it becomes the language of commerce.

July 1

A run on the hill. A cicada shell blown by the wind, tumbling along the ground. I got worn down by the wind, but well worn. Wear the philosophy out of me, dear God, put cicadas, rocks, wind in its place. That awful, blustery dryness, the raw hillside. Then, a cholla blossom, scarlet in the middle of infinite brown. We need rain. The deerflies are bad. The mosquitoes are bad. The cicadas are mechanical. They have no sense of themselves or where they are going. Their bodies are a dumb burden, something for the only slightly more intelligent wings to carry around. The cicadas must be cycling this summer: are they five-year cicadas? thirteen-year cicadas? Books can't tell me what I need to know about cicadas, but by telling me everything but, they help reveal the need. I took a wrong turn on the way down and found myself on a hostile ridge, bare-shouldered, gravelly earth, nowhere to go, so I went back. Usually I don't approve of going back.

Two people testing each other out. Each with needs that will or will not be compromised. Will we live together or apart? A little apart, or altogether apart?

July 2
Things are changing, I'm changing, but I can't seem to change fast enough to keep up with the things. Stayed up until midnight, and when I got up, the sun was already lying on top of me, warm and steady. Molly's going away sooner than expected. To Austin, first, to see her parents. Wonderful sunshine. I am wonderfully alone. The trick is to let nothing keep you down, to keep driving at whatever small truth you can get at, no matter how many times it beats you back and denies you. Better yet, like watching birds, sit very still and let it come to you. Just stay put.

July 6
Absence. An absence. Imagining her return, saying, "I couldn't have done it without you." Thoughts of marriage, married people. My father, the most devoutly married man the world has known, telling me in confidence, "I think a man could live just as happily without ever getting married." The implication was that a woman couldn't. Who or what is absent?

They broke into Delio's store again: "They took bread, eggs, bacon, all the bubble gum I had."

Nighthawks. I sat outside while it was getting dark and watched them write essays on the insect life of the area. "Area" has become one of Hannah's words: "I already swept this area." Things happen all around me, but what is happening to me? I am all things, a housewife, a working mother. I want to be a woman and see the world as a woman sees it, as Molly would see it if she were here. Tonight, I walked the garden as she would, drinking coffee, pulling pigweed.

And what if poems were nothing more than a loving observation of all things, a noticing and an offering up? "Take, eat, this is my body."

The day before she left I killed the guineas. I did it in the morning with an axe. I don't know why I did it. I said it was because they were bullying the chickens but I think I did it because it would spoil her going away, so that even when she had gone she couldn't be completely gone; a part of her would have to stay here to grieve for her birds. Hannah said, "You can't kill the guineas. Life is life."

The young cottonwood by the river, heavy with seed, a girl who is about to know her first love. The young girl, suddenly old enough. Too suddenly. I look in her eyes: one day she does not know what I am thinking, the next she does.

What makes us sing? The nighthawks. The water coming to a boil.

Marriage isn't a thing to be liked or disliked, believed in or not believed in. It's more like a collection of works, each different, a constant working towards and a leaving behind. The last sentence, the last stroke of the brush. It's never quite what you expected but you come to a point when you just have to leave it alone, leave it be. The next one, we say, will be better.

July 7
Philatropy: faithfulness to the previous home area (in birds).

Common nighthawk. How can anything that flies be common?

Gray this morning. My eyes see rain, but it isn't raining.

Eat. Wash the dishes. Sweep. Wash the clothes. Feed the animals. Tie the shoes. Brush the hair. If not here, where? Comfort in duty, convention. But more than convention. Ceremony. The season of your not being here. Everything withers and blooms. I don't know where the year is taking me. I am at once more sufficient and more helpless than ever before. Try to imagine what good will come of it. What good work will come of this being apart? The song of lonesome me. The song of home and the coffee pot and the eggs in their egg-shaped holes in the refrigerator. Drip-system emitters: small hissing lives under the green leaves. I hate weeding but I do it anyway because the weeds have something to tell us. Song of the helpless husband. Women find nothing endearing or interesting in helplessness. I will find new ways of breaking eggs, whole new ways of being helpless.

July 8
Oklahoma lady at work yesterday, observing new porch: "What happened?" This is the correct thing to say where she's from, to express surprise and admiration. Another complimentary convention of speech in the West: you offer to steal someone's children.

[196]

Mrs. Trujillo brings me Kool-Aid. Mr. Trujillo calls her "the chief of police."

July 9
I got sunburnt, and on my lips, I put the ointment for nursing mothers. Will my speech be like cream?

July 10
Hannah: "I won't let you get turkey skin like Grandpa Bernie. Do all peoples get turkey skin? Delio gots turkey skin. A little."

Early in the morning, I walk through the garden tearing the heads off the dill, spilling the seed. She said it has a tendency to get rank. My cousins, the socks; the political jeans.

July 11
Last night I hung the wash out on the line, none of her parts left in there to hang except a couple of feet. At least there were plenty of clothespins for a change. My fingers were quick on the pins, I was virtuous.

July 12
Butchered chickens. The soccer game on TV, like the rest of the day, without passion. The president of Italy beamed and waved, but he didn't really mean it. He didn't really want to kiss those other dignitaries after the victory on their fat white dignified cheeks, but he did it anyway. The kids made a love potion, which at least killed the smell of the chickens. Even the emotional

Italians were not emotional enough, not even in their black shirts and long black curls. A shot of the Italian coach: Jim McKay says, "Don't you think he's emotionally involved?" On the possiblity of leaving La Madera, Michael said, "I feel like you're already gone." The neighbors sat on the porch and watched us chase chickens. What was it about this day? The inconvenience of raising and butchering chickens, not worth the meat on their bones? But not just that. Everything seemed too much trouble. I wasn't there, like Michael said, I had already gone someplace else. The kids had the right idea: a pinch of this, a tablespoon of that, making love.

July 13

So many die young here. Now Facundo, dead of bubonic plague. He was running a fever for a while, didn't think anything of it, and by the time they got him to the hospital it was too late. So full of life, to be done in by a flea.

Mouse in the cabinet. Lizard in the bathtub. Hannah grabbed him and put him outside, then another, imaginary one.

Every so often I imagine living here in La Madera, but as another man living in another country, someone whose acquaintance I would like to make. But the imaginary man is too sure of himself, too comfortable. After a while, we have nothing to say to each other.

July 15

I saw a flashy caterpillar climbing the dill. Hannah saw "a white moth with white spots." She wanted to walk towards the people, I wanted to walk away from them. I said, "Go ahead, you go that way and I'll go this way." One of these days she'll call my bluff.

The things that swell up your lymph glands with bubonic plague are called bubos. Starting in Constantinople in 1334, it killed three-quarters of the population of Europe and Asia.

July 16
Hannah sleeps downstairs. I sleep in one of three places, my bed, hers, or downstairs, sometimes all three in one night. When I'm working outside she sits on her swing, dawdling her toes, thinking about what? Last night we took a little walk and I sang "Clementine." "That's a sad song, huh, Tom?"

Summer advances. The freezer's on the blink. Hannah sleeps. Since it's so dry here and so wet in Tennessee, she wants to know why we can't go to Tennessee and have rain.

Six geese running with their wings hung out. Hard wind, a few drops of rain. Every leaf showing its pale green underside: Marilyn Monroe in effigy, her dress lifted forever and ever at an amusement park called Stars Over Gatlinburg.

July 18
I'm the house's wife. Put a broom in my hands, I'm happy. Leroy the refrigerator man is coming. When I turned the freezer off last night, the house fell strangely, wonderfully silent. Hannah wakes. Mozart simplifies things. Waiting for Leroy the refrigerator man. When all else fails, sweep. Sweep the house, the porch, the lawn, the ditches. A hummingbird rattles outside the door, or is it the death rattle of our dying freezer? Sometimes art is just a further

complication of what seems too complicated to begin with; but sometimes, as in the case of Mozart, it uncomplicates. Hannah's favorite ladybug's name is Allergy. We had a very grownup discussion today about how you could tell what coyotes eat by examining their spoor. It's all right to pick it up, yes. This coyote was eating cicadas, or maybe grasshoppers, you could see the shining bits of their wings. Two rocks, one on either side of the road, each marked with a blue arrow pointing that way. The cowboys at the top of the ridge gave me a beer. People are like geese: if you aren't afraid of them you have nothing to fear. What a cool relief, when shyness falls away. We came down off the mountain in a downpour. Rain breaks the back of our remorse. The immeasureable green meadow and three Spanish cowboys: not the thing that reminds you of other things, other times, other people dead or alive, but just the thing, free of memory and remorse. The hermit thrush wasn't the one I used to hear on the fringes of aspen wood. It was a new one. Gathering yarrow: to hell with the future. Instead, the smell of yarrow, broken away from its high green ground. The cleanliness, the sapience of aspen. The ease of their limbs. A pair of calves on the road in the rain. Do they mind the rain? Do they ever think, "It's raining"? Hannah wants to know which are the boys and which are the girls. Cows have bags and bulls have balls except the ones that don't, but she's not listening, she's watching the rain. The sound in the trees is more like the river than the wind. Molly would like this or that, wouldn't she? She would. Why did they use yarrow and none other to reveal circumstances, which after all are only circumstances and obvious, if we could only see them. But the plant itself must have some special and unmysterious quality to do that. Hermit? A hermit is a person who goes off by himself to be alone. A hermit thrush is a certain kind of a bird that doesn't hang around with other birds. A robin is a kind of thrush. Say it. Thrush. Are you happy for the rain? Yes. Happy for the happiness that the rain knows when it's falling.

Leroy the refrigerator man looks like a refrigerator. His wife came along for the ride. She knows a little Spanish, but only the bad words, and teaches her Spanish friends to cuss in Indian. "You've got a good box," says Leroy. "These older boxes in my experience you got to work with them."

North wind tonight, first thought of winter. My father's annual report arrives in photocopy, still getting by on Chief Liquid Assets. It's all right to love, but don't love too much. Hang back. Let the loved one come to you. So, we calculate ourselves to death and love's lost in the very thought of not having it. A sweet, cool breeze tonight. The freezer is making a fool of itself, like an old man with a new lover. Go to bed.

July 19
The freezer's still running. The harder I work, the more my bank account stays the same. Rain during the night, and the smell of winter. Thoughts of a strange room in a city, drippy gypsy violin, burnt tortillas.

July 22
Morning. Tiny spider scaling invisible thread, up into the lampshade. Felt bad all day yesterday. Mopped the floor. The dump was overrun by slow (bubonic?) gray squirrels. Warning on post office door: PLAGUE. Any animal slow enough to catch may have it.

July 23

Getting to know the weeds. Red-ribbed sucker weed. Rampant megalomania weed. Volunteer okay weed. I feel austerity coming on, but oh, the burden of desire and the heaviness of late July. Reading the ancient Chinese text, I want to be nothing but a gardener and a keeper of birds. Lately, the barn swallows have been swinging by, potential tenants. The weeds can hear me coming when I'm pulling weeds. This one knows its being looked at, judged. In its favor, small, dry orange flowers. Go ahead, live, see if I care.

July 29

Last night, with an orange for the sun and a tennis ball for the earth, Hannah and I learned why it gets dark earlier in Tennessee. We live on a great round ball that turns. Here's mom and here's us. There's the sun coming up. It doesn't really come up, though. The earth turns and it just looks like it's coming up. It might seem like we're staying in one place but everything's really turning, and the way you can tell it's turning is the sun coming up. We live on a great round ball that goes around two ways at once but you can't feel it. Except when you get dizzy, says Hannah.

Charles Ives would run away from a conversation to jot down a few bars of music, or rush home from the office. But he never complained about having to work for a living. In a note to his copyist, he remarked, "Mr. Price: Please don't try to make things nice! All the wrong notes are right."

In a windstorm, Hannah stuck out her arms like wings. The wind caught her and lifted her. I remembered a story my mother told, how one day when she was a girl walking home from school a big wind came. She was afraid she would be blown away like a candy wrapper, so she held tight to an elm tree, hugged it for all she was worth and cried. Hannah came running to me in this wind, her hair curled by the rain, shouting, "I flew! I flew!"

Clouds against the mountain this morning, I sat in a chair on the east side of the house and watched. This is a beautiful place but sometimes you have to move your chair to see it a different way, sit in a place you haven't before, make yourself sit in awareness and newness here on the east side, where you go to do certain things like turning on the water but where you never have gone just to sit and muse.

Why people get fat: they lose their desire. When we are young we are thin because we want so much, we are constantly impoverished. When we get older we get fat because we have things or think we have them and do not want as much. Merton said the holiest man is the one who wants the most, not the one who is the most satisfied.

All this summer, the feeling that I ought to be getting ready to do something, then the conviction that I was already doing it, that there was nothing more important or fulfilling to be done than cook tortillas and feed the chickens.

Threw a ching. *Chien,* difficulty.

July 30
Yesterday in thunder and lightning, one of the turkeys gobbled for

the first time. Woke early. Anxieties. We will not live in Chimayo because if I'm going to carpenter I can do it better here and if Molly's going to help with money she can't do it any better in Chimayo than here. In most families, I suppose the job determines everything, where you will be, what kind of place you live in, where your children go to school, what kind of water you drink. Fear: getting stuck in the city, paying big rent, for what? Fear: leaving La Madera just as I am beginning to be somebody here, one of the people. Fear: we won't be able to find a renter or a place to rent. Molly on the telephone: "You can't imagine how remote all these problems seem to me."

July 31
To wake in the dark and peel off the skins of your dream; to go out in the dark in the wet yard where drops of water hang from the asparagus berries and the night sounds are swamp sounds, sounds of water. And this our dry land smells like water and the creek runs brown. My daughter is sleeping. Will I ever know her again the way I know her now, just the two of us against the world, against each other? In times to come she will tolerate her offbeat father and make jokes about him, no sisters to giggle with, but friends. She will have an abundance of friends, not like me, no backward, tight-mouthed recluse. And this place. Will I have to be remembering it, trying to reconstruct this wet dawn somewhere else? How did the day smell? What was I feeling? And when I try to say just what it is I'm feeling and how the morning feels, all I can come up with is the rain, and other early mornings when the pavement or the earth was wet. Where? Cambridge? And why didn't I write those times down and make something of them? Take hold, don't

let them go by, don't wait for ripeness or maturity or wisdom or opportunity any longer. What was it Molly wrote? Go for broke. Wet morning. The square root of minus one on the calculator: trying to foul up the circuitry, the certainty of my life. The salvation of error. Wet mornings, wet dawns. Coffee and sweet rolls, being awake, hearing the single log truck. This morning I got up before him. Airports. Suspension of life between here and there, and old Tom Merton, sweet Tom on the train, the Orient Express, seeing that woman washing her clothes. That's it! Water buffalos! Helicopter yesterday. See the strange large bird? Hannah's eyes get big, then she gets the joke. "Oh, Tom." Molly's letter to her: the popcorn machine, popcorn jumping on the floor in rainy Tennessee, but not so precious as this rain, the roosters not as excellent as mine, who are just now learning to crow and their voices make me think of the smell of joss sticks because *things mean things:* the rooster means incense, and the helicopter means searching the river for the body of a dead man, and I deceive myself that at eight o'clock this morning the *real* work will begin. Things mean things: the substance of faith, what we live for, those meanings, those coincidences of sky & rain & thought that jump at us.

I asked Hannah permission to freeze her rooster along with the rest of them. Life is life, she told me. Me, her own father. "Life is life," she said. "You can't just throw it away."

August 1
Old man Mauro's grapes will not ripen until September. I asked him how to make wine. "That's the easiest thing there is to do," he said. "Mash em up good, ferment em, drain em off. Make a wine,

that's the easiest thing there is. Show you? I don't have to show you." Later on, he calls to me from across the fence: "Here, boy, can you catch?" Tosses over a big, ripe apricot.

Trying to pick out the best crower to save for the hens. But if I move, how will I ever take the crowing with me?

Washing Hannah's hair. How she screams and hollers! How sweet and clean and obedient she is when it's done! Saying, in these very words, "I'll do anything you tell me to do."

Don't get organized. Just get. Sometime within the last few days, the season did a turnaround. Started to rain, started to feel like woodsmoke. Getting through the summer. We made it! More of an accomplishment, even, than getting through February.

August 4
The mercy of crows. When the field's cut, they find new interest in it, bathe in the ditches, squabble with each other. The mathematical set of thoughts had while the water comes to a boil, the bucket fills, the moon comes up.

After Hannah's nightmare:
    "Don't be afraid. Dreams aren't real."
    "But what about the wooden nurses?"

August 6
The rotten peach on Molly's desk in Gatlinburg: like the world seen from outer space. Where does outer space end and inner space begin? The absence: good or bad? Molly sees herself in a mirror, neither wife nor mother nor daughter, for it wasn't very long

ago we languished under the supervision of parents, the comfort and tyranny of home. The absence reveals the being together: how we succumb to habit, avoid risk in everyday things, fall asleep on the couch, gravitate to that warm center which is the family and which sometimes keeps us from our explorations, the "lost and undiscovered." How renew ourselves at that warm center so it does not imprison us?

Mud plastering the house, which Molly first plastered five years ago by hand. I showed Hannah the prints of her mother's hand on the wall, still clearly visible, pocked by driving rain. I plastered over the old mud with a trowel, burying her finger rainbows, her ups and downs, her flourishes. Where the old mud ended and the new mud began, I could read her and me. Me: hard, clean edges, places worried over with the trowel. Her: uncalculated, unedited grace, but more than that, and what I envy most, the fearlessness, the going ahead.

Sometimes I take a cowardly refuge in the journal, the way the man and the woman take a cowardly refuge in each other from their work that wants to be done, that must be done even in the midst of cooking, washing, sweeping the floor. What we are asking for ourselves may be unreasonable, and yet we are asking for it. How much easier just to be married, make a home, make money, watch the children grow, be joyful. Easy or impossible? Instead, we have made our joy depend on our work, and having come this far we can't renounce it, can't be free from it, but only look for freedom in it. But if the absence has been so good for us, what are we doing together? If we are to be together, it comes back to this: to be more alone together than we could ever be apart, enforcing one another's solitudes; to be, her wish for me, our heart's desire.

August 7
"Mom was going to come home today but she got stuck in Mrs. Hippy."

Storm coming. Just throw the mud on the wall. Don't get too fine with the trowel. Just keep putting it on until there's no art to it, just work. Finally today, after days of plastering, I came to a point through whatever it was — fatigue, relaxation, being tired of old ways, sick of habitual movements — that I put the mud on with assurance, and began to let the trowel do things I had not let it do before: half circles, ridges, and their *reverberations* on return strokes. What was Ives's phrase? Shadow rhythms ["shadow counterpoint"]. Then when it's all done, step back to see what you've done. Out of the randomness, an order emerges, but you can't make it and you can't prevent it.

St. Francis fasted forty days, ate half a loaf of bread to save himself from pride. It doesn't say if he enjoyed the half. Perfect joy: have someone beat you with a knotty club.

Chairs turned upside down on the tops of tables, floors smelling of Lysol.

Rain cools the world. I stand outside watching the swallows. Hannah observes butterflies, I promise her a net. White-breasted nuthatch on the juniper. The world and how it makes me feel, these tastes of despair like metal on the tongue, those seizures of god-strewn joy. There must be someone in these hills who knows how to cut hair, who can take all this heaviness from me. Among the things I would like to give up: those mercurial wings that grow behind my ears.

When I stand outside watching the clouds and the birds, I'm doing my work. These things need to be studied and praised, at least reported on. I moved the last three cocks into the isolation cell; at the moment the cell door closed, the one who had been chosen to live, the cockadoodledoo rooster, the one who sounds most the way a rooster ought to sound, crowed. He had not crowed since we put him back in with the hens a few days ago — the hens abuse him — but when he saw the other roosters helpless, held upside down by the mastering hand, the coward crowed: "I am the rooster! I am the rooster!"

Frank: two holes in his heart, his flesh withered, his bare leg swollen and red as if if someone had turned it over a fire. Bankrupt, all their belongings priced for sale, all the neighbors stopping by to survey the wreckage of their lives. I looked at the books and bought one that had been in the rain, a window broken by vandals had let the rain in, and the book is growing mildew, the beginning of corruption. Books, like people, are perishable.

Is this time apart a hardship? A privilege? My mother sends her wisdom: may you have great sadness and great joy. Dark night. No music. No guns. Hannah has a rash. Freezer will not stop running. Found a flea on Franklin. In the morning, it will all seem much less forbidding. I do fine without Molly. Do I do better without her? What's it for, anyway, this cleaving unto one another? Who needs it? Why all the trouble, the worry, the compromise? Is it possible for two people to make things actually *easier* on each other? I don't miss the television. I have satanized it, societal decadence and all that, cause and symptom rolled into one.

I live here, I am one of the odd little people who have come here to live, the ones who came much odder than the natives. Doc Daniels, who pulled out his thick roll of cash and bought all of my eggs in one grand, smiling gesture, as if he would have bought twenty dozen instead of three if I'd had them. Beth at the Roadrunner, who says we run into one another in "odd little places." And Lalo with his amphibious fingers and dashed dreams of glory as a thoroughbred jockey. I live here too, now. I am one of them. What kind of man would take three dozen eggs for a ride in the pickup on the chance of peddling them by the roadside? "We don't buy eggs anymore, huh, Tom? We lay them." The town is crossing the river, taking me in. Or maybe it's me that's getting closer to it. Now I see the bad boys and think, uh huh, there's me, I could be a bad boy too. They don't scare me any more. Who's the gringo who walks into town for his mail? The gringo who lives in the house with the tin roof at La Junta: somebody at last, although the closest I could ever really come to being somebody here is if Hannah grew up and married a local man and had a child, which would make me, if not exactly somebody, than somebody's grandfather. What's the use of being somebody, anyway? Poor Frank. Sickness and misfortune may bring us at last to the right god. The freezer won't turn off; like me, just barely holding its own, too heavy to carry out of the house.

August 8
Bluegrass lyric:

This summer I went swimming
This summer I might have drowned
But I held my breath
And I kicked my feet
And I moved my arms around.

To dive down, Gilgamesh has to tie rocks to his feet, so strong-minded, so buoyant a man is he. At the bottom, he seizes the plant that will give everlasting life but it cuts his hand and he sees his blood flow into the water. And yesterday Hannah stepped barefoot on a cactus. I heard her screams and thought, these are not screams of delight, and yet I waited for the wet towel to finish going through the wringer before I ran to see what had happened.

A vision of life in the city: Roshi! Here I am at last! I fall at his feet, weeping. My clothes are all clean and sweet smelling. My food is clean. I hardly have to eat at all. The mornings fill with clean, cool sunlight. A sad flute plays on the stereo. There aren't any animals. My wife sees me with new desire and draws me down to her on the clean linoleum. My daughter plays the cello and speaks a dozen languages. My car isn't rusty.

August 9
When Molly comes back, will we be the same people, or will we be somebody else?

August 10
First brush of fall, the squawberry turns red, the rufous humming-

bird loses interest in the hollyhocks. Big rain, the kind that scares you with the bigness of its waters, the sky all like a river coming down. I was on the roof today, thinking about lightning. I took the stovepipe apart and cleaned it and I didn't cuss once. Captured a black swallowtail, killed it with mothballs, which seems like a terribly slow death. The wings of moths and butterflies do not endure human touch.

Man and woman: must they dull each other's creative edge, or can they sharpen each other, blade and steel?

August 13
Hannah fast asleep, eyes open, looking at me. Tomorrow Molly calls to say when she's coming home. Picking tomato hornworms: I'd rather tangle with a mountain lion. You think you've already found the biggest one, but there's always a bigger one yet to find. You can be looking right at it and see nothing but the vegetable tomato when before your very eyes it turns to green animal flesh.

Another uncomfortable experience: the black swallowtail that I put in the killing jar two days ago and mounted on a pin came fully back to life and was flopping around trying to get loose. I had to do some fast talking when Hannah asked, "How could it get alive again?" By now it's so battered and abused that it's not even worth keeping. So much for amateur biology. Left alone, the butterfly was like an idea; killing and mounting it was like a corruption of the idea, an overwriting of it. When it flew close, the inevitability of its landing there among the blossoms by the gate; but also, and at the same time, the impossibility of it.

This longing for god takes place in the context of the commonest things, home and family, which are both help and hindrance. Does salvation come up out of the ground or down out of the sky? I look up, bird-crazed; Molly looks down, to growing things; we are as different as earth and sky. She reminds me to watch my step.

Tony Maroni and his gang came looking for their lost white goat, or at least that's what they said they were looking for. He came in without knocking; a toad came in with him, but I don't think they were together.

The rain barrel and its questions: is it better to be full, or capable of being filled; wise, or ready to receive wisdom?

August 14
House for rent La Madera $200/month plus utilities.

August 16
Elvis Presley died five years ago today. Thousands gather in Memphis.

August 17
The day before the last day. I have not been waiting for her to come back all summer, but now I'm waiting (someone wrote a poem called "Patience Is When You Stop Waiting" [C. K. Williams]). Am I older? Six weeks is not such a long time, but who is coming home to me, and who will she find? If not her husband, who?

Big lightning & rainstorm. Those big bolts coming straight down to earth. The sound of ripping, torn atmosphere, the world getting sucked through a pipe, falling bombs. Clytie's ram lamb, crying all

[215]

night long, still crying for his mother.

Will I suffer by comparison to all that stimulation, the crack of creation, the impossibility of sleep? What kind of woman can get by on six hours of sleep a night? Not mine. My own sweet daughter descends. Fix the breakfast, says she. How can you fix what's not broken?

The world's record for continuous Pac-Man play (32 hours) was set yesterday in Roswell, New Mexico, in an electronic game emporium on Main Street called Playland. Some kid beat a hardened Air Force man. Meanwhile, work goes on at the Pentagon. Leave them alone, boys will be boys.

If I forget everybody's birthday, then nobody will be left out.

The rain barrel: I didn't want the rain as much as I wanted to contain it.

Hannah: "I know what you said, I want to know *what you were going to say.*" That's what I'm after: the thing that was about to be said, intended to be said, but didn't, couldn't, wouldn't. The thing we forgot and go on forgetting.

Hannah, mad at me: "The girl flies don't eat shit, do they, Tom? Only the boys." Awake at half past four, my light the only light in all the valley, and all the insects in the valley trying to get at it. I have woken the flies and given the moths a new lease on life. I have my new ways, too. Molly will not be the only one who needs to adjust, who needs a space and a time to work. How will I learn again to make coffee for two? Coffee for one is so convenient, and supper's ready right now. Rain. Waiting, speaking of rain. I took the sheep across to separate the ram; a flood came down the river, now they can't get back across. Only the boy flies eat shit. Stepping outside, inevitably overwhelmed, tossed overboard by something new, usually the sky. Like my father, I am much taken with the sky; in most things, I am conscientiously opposed to his values, but sometimes, I just can't help it, I am helplessly taken by the sky. My father had a hammer. I never saw him drive a nail, but I never saw him throw it at anybody, either.

Molly delayed. The suspense is keeping me alive.

August 20
Hannah and I return from Santa Fe without Molly, who says she doesn't want to live here anymore. Now, however, we are complete without her, where before, someone was missing. Hannah fell asleep this afternoon, and when she woke, she thought it was morning and she had missed breakfast. She thought I was fooling and kept on doggedly insisting that the sun was coming up and kept on calling this morning yesterday. Then it got dark.

Making butter. This must have been how the universe was made. God pushed the puree button on his Osterizer, stars, planets, galaxies curdled out of nothingness, and he dipped them out with a wooden spoon.

I keep thinking, this is a great time for us. I was going to give Molly some of my thoughts on absence, write them up and make her a present, but now I have to keep thinking them.

August 24

Hannah's first day of kindergarten. She stands by the gate until the bus comes, looks both ways to see if anything is coming, crosses the road. The bus looks big compared to her from where I am standing down in the field with a white bucket. As big as it looks to her, maybe even bigger. I go back up to the house to see what time the bus came. 8:20 a.m. The white bucket stands by the door, and I can't remember what I was going to do with it. The Lapetacabus, she called it, one word, name of a mythical beast. It came around the corner from La Petaca, yellow lights flashing. She's never been on a big bus before. It stops, the door opens. She gets in without any hesitation, without looking to see if I am there seeing her get on the schoolbus all by herself for the first time. The bus crosses the bridge, makes the turn at Tony's, disappears. I'm alone. The white bucket stands by the door, and I wonder, was it supposed to have something in it?

Never mind what's missing. Remember what's here and available, what's been given: this place, these creatures. The geese are on the river, the young ones almost as big as the parents now. Sometimes, on the water, or in the middle of the night, they cry out in some kind of passion.

FAREWELL, FLESH: A STORY

It was July — a hot, windless afternoon when the cicadas made a noise all together like fat frying in a skillet, and almost everyone who didn't have to be out was in. Down by the river, down below the mirage of corrugated steel roofs, the ditch where the spearmint grew, the tidy orchards and the long alleys of hayland, down past the wide, tall, leafy park where the big alamos dropped their dead limbs and cows stared thickly from their caves in the gooseberry bushes, Tony Alire the Senior woke from his nap without admitting to himself that he had been asleep, and saw that if he did not move the sun would soon come out of the branches and fall on him. The river was way down, and clear, the way mineral oil is clear. Invisible things floated there — the residue of bathing birds? the torn wing of a damselfly? The shadows of these things squirmed across the bottom.

On most afternoons as hot as this one he would be sitting on his back porch and Amelia would be starting to think about supper. Neighbors driving by would look for his spanking white Panama, the one he'd bought in Nuevo Laredo on their second honeymoon even though she said it made him look like a coffee broker. They'd look for him among the rampant greens of Amelia's porch plants. They'd wave, and he'd wave slowly, grandly back.

But today Amelia was visiting her sister in Albuquerque, breathing the unhealthy air of an air conditioner and drinking sugared drinks while her sister's husband, no relation to Tony worth naming, squatted in the infernal backyard heat and cooked hamburgers to death on a hibachi.

He would have none of it. He would have the cathedral solitude of the river bosque, nerves of sunlight filtering through the cottonwoods, the secret womanless pools where he had fished since he was a boy, the shock of a trout taking the fly, the firm halves turned in cornmeal and so lightly broiled that when he parted the flesh with his fork, there would be pinkness yet, and a faint whiff of the Rio Sapillo.

Where he had slept in deep shade, he woke now at the edge of heat, and felt for his hat. It wasn't there. He smoothed back the sweaty confusion of his hair, which lay all on top of his head in swirls and counterswirls. The hat had fallen unharmed into the leaf mold: El Gaucho Size M, white as a virgin hen. He put it back on, and considered the sun's advances. If he were to catch any fish today, he would have to be catching them, for at best he was a daytime fisherman, and did not get along with the swarms of mosquitoes that would come in the late afternoon.

His rod rested in the crook of an alder. His line, clotted with algae, made a G clef on the surface of the stream. When he started to reel in, he knew there was something on the other end. He knew this even before the line went taut and he could feel the dull drag of something not dead, but dead for all practical purposes, and inedible besides — a drag familiar to him in recent summers but not in summers long gone when the Rio Sapillo ran cold and the suckers had not yet moved in. They would get on your hook not out of any true hunger, he was convinced, but out of stupid curiosity, and stay there without fighting because they did not even have enough life in them to know they had been caught. Or they'd swim into the ditch when it was full and belly into the wet fields, grounding themselves in the high places and curling their luster-less tails out of the water until the field dried up and they were left to the mercy of crows — soft, bony, muddy-tasting things that only a crow or a man much poorer than himself could stomach.

The sucker was hooked bloodlessly through its upper lip. It watched Tony remove the hook without any apparent malice, fear, or pain. He slapped its head against a rock and tossed it to the cattails.

"Good riddance to bad rubbish."

He freed his troutfly, and snapped it back into its own plastic pillbox. Others, the trusted and the scorned, creatures of thread and feather, of iridescent plumes from the throat of a Rhode Island rooster, of pink Dow-Corning insulation, of fake pearl buttons, rovings and laces and sequins swiped from Amelia's sewing basket, of odds and ends from dusty drawers in Rael's Mercantile that had been there so long that even Rael didn't know what they were — all lived in the tackle box, a condominium for spiders when he wasn't gone fishing. No, not in his hat, even though it had a wide blue band with Sonoran javelinas on it, chasing one another eternally around his head. He might have kept his flies in his hat if Amelia had not been waiting so eagerly for it to discolor or disintegrate or otherwise fall into sin so she could throw it away. Tony kept his flies where they belonged.

The rod was of fiberglass, the collapsible kind. By the time he broke it down into its three irreducible lengths and tied it back together with the same pieces of baling twine that he always tied it with, the sun was blasting its full demon strength on him, and he retreated into the still, open spaces of the bosque. He walked along whistling "Un Amor Tan Maravilloso," an old favorite, thinking about a bear he had killed when he was younger. A big cinnamon bear, a she. And fat? When they skinned it and hung it up in a tree, it was as white as a sheet on Amelia's line.

All at once La Pascualita stood in his path where she certainly had not been a moment before, her face as quick as a bird's and as wild, scanning the treetops for hawkish shapes of death. In no way did she acknowledge his coming. She wore a red goosedown vest — goosedown, on this, the most infernal day of summer — a gray woolen schoolgirl's jumper over a purple leotard, tennis sneakers, and in her long, gray hair, a trio of purple asters, the kind that bloomed along the highway. She shouldered her broom like a carbine, and when he gave her the old greeting ("God give you a good day, Señora Maestas.") she gave the treetops a look of mean approval.

La Pascualita was a woman of the town, its custodian and its ward. Most of the time you would see her sweeping the highway, an endless task, God help her, and one for which she received no pay, no home of her own or husband to cook for, but only the spare beds of the townspeople and the extra chair at their tables. She would go along the centerstripe with the slow, certain progress of a sheep pulling grass, pausing now and then to mop the sweat from her brow, to look back at what had already been swept or ahead at what was left. She would be smiling if she had been treated well at the last house, scowling if she had not. Good or bad, she was treated like family, even though she had none of her own that anybody cared to remember. Whenever she wore out a broom, they would take a collection in church and buy her a new one.

"And you, Antonio Alire," she said with the voice of one who has forgotten herself. "God give you a good day, too."

La Pascualita had not always been the way she was. People said she was once the most beautiful girl in the village, but somehow, she had never grown into the most beautiful woman. They said she'd run away with a carnival man when she was fifteen, and ever after that, though she was still beautiful, and functioning in her body the way a woman functions, she wasn't quite right. They said it was the carnival man who'd wrenched her mind out of place and made her unfit for a wife.

In the summers, so long ago that hardly anyone alive could remember (and maybe even they were telling what they had been told), the *maramores* would travel north out of Old Mexico, beating their drums and tambourines, stopping in every plaza along the way to put on a show. Once there had been dancing dogs in the village of El Sapillo — dancing dogs in pinafores, it was said, and a woman who could double over backwards and stick her head between her legs so it looked like she was giving birth to an enormous, hairy child; and a man, a beautiful brown Mexican who flew the trapeze right there in the plaza where Rael's gas pumps now stood. He told La Pascualita that he would teach her how to fly the trapeze, too. It was he, they said, who'd made her the way she was, and in place of some firm, kind, working man put the dead handle of a broom.

Tony did not stop to chat. He liked being there, in the river bottom, where no one would have gone on a day this hot but someone like himself, a sportsman and a man of nature, down where there were no willows to sting your cheek or cargos of ripening seed to get in your socks. He liked being alone, and invisible to all the world of people who would expect him to linger and talk. So what if he'd only caught a sucker? Fish, as any fisherman knows, aren't what you go fishing for anyway.

He climbed the cobbled bank where the cholla cactus had opened in full magenta glory and the ants were busy tiling the roof of their ant hill with thousands of little round stones. If you looked very carefully, the way his uncle Celso always had the patience to look when he was alive, you might even find a tiny turquoise bead among the other ant pebbles — fashioned by an ancient hand, lost and buried, exposed again by the rain and dragged up on the hill by some poor slaving insect who had not the slightest inkling that this stone was any better than the rest. No bead caught Tony's eye, but that was all right. Things like searching for treasure and fishing were meant to answer desires of the spirit, not the flesh.

Irrigation water leaked out of the field into the arroyo. The frothy green pillows of algae that clung to rocks would have felt like the lungs of a freshly killed beef, had he felt them. But his affection for things of the earth went just so far and no farther, embraced toad but not snake; owl but not buzzard; liver but not lung. His galoshes made such a noise in the wet field that he scared off a pair of crows that had been squabbling over something. They flew off towards the dump screaming "carne! carne!" So it pleased him to think. The sun was getting so steamy hot that he took a place by the fence, over in the shade of the plum trees with their brand-new powdery green plums. The crows circled over the dump, and seeing that nothing dead had been left while they were away, returned and landed plop down in the field without any concern for the man who sat in the shade of the plum trees. Crows know people by their luggage. A fishing rod, especially one that has been broken in two places and rests on the ground, cannot do harm.

La Pascualita stepped through the wet grass holding her sneakers up daintily, as if the water might suddenly rise up and confiscate them.

"Carne!" said the crows, and flapped off into the hills.

She came sloshing up to Tony where he sat and pointed a finger in his direction. She would not look him full in the eye, no more than she would look at any man. To do so would be to show the depth of her sorrow. It would leap out and show itself to other people and then who would she be? If such a thing ever happened to La Pascualita she would surely die, and all that would be left would be an old lady who'd known but one man in her life, who'd had no goodness from him, and who in her ancient days could not even claim the holy distinction of virginity. How great Our Lady's longing must have been, to suffer all the hardships of being a wife and mother, and never know that single, annihilating shock of joy! The women of the town would kneel in church and weep to think of it.

But Pascualita. Poor old Pascualita with her broom, who had nothing sensible to say but would sometimes stop in the middle of the road to say it, laying her instrument down carefully on the centerstripe and throwing her small, unspotted hands in circles until the thing was said and she could go on down the road — poor old Pascualita had neither man nor God to fill her up, and had to make do with the unsanctioned spirits that were said to follow her everywhere, protecting her from the log trucks that barrelled down out of the mountains, listening to her middle-of-the-road speeches, and ushering her unspoiled to the next night's lodging.

She stood ankle deep in water looking at nothing in particular, the way a man who goes to catch a spooky horse will look at nothing in particular to disguise his intentions. She stood so still that her spirits, had they been visible, would have come to rest in the air around her and not told jokes or lit cigarettes or rustled their chemises, just to show their respect for La Pascualita's stillness.

Then in an instant she was on her knees in the water, her sneakers and her broom cast off from her, staring with astonishment at the two empty hands which in that instant had held the fish so firmly. A spirit fish. It had made itself incorporeal just long enough to get away, then jumped back into its body and skittered away. With a body and a tail and enough water to move them in, it might yet find its way back to the river, its beloved stagnancies. Tomorrow it might yet slide its fat lips across the rocks, stir the filth from the bottom, breed in its own good time.

Pascualita seized her broom and started to sweep. Her spirits broke into an uproar. They cackled and squealed and snapped each other's brassieres, urging her to sweep, sweep the fertile haylands clean, sweep all the dross and foulness out of them, sweep for the great taking in of fall and the great eating of winter. She swept with a fury, but swept well. Her broom swept neatly around the sweet blades of timothy and gently over young clover. She swept all the bad things before her, things that in no way belong in a field of hay.

The fish, mothers and calves and a few golden bulls, swam faster than they ever had in their dull lives, fleeing before La Pascualita's broom. She slapped the water with the flat of it, scanned the spreader ditches like a Miami retiree with a metal detector. She charged up and down, striking the surface with her flinty old heels and wetting herself, but good. The generations of suckers crowded against the irrigation levee. In their fright, they climbed on one another's backs, or screwed their heads into the mud so they wouldn't have to look.

Que no quiero verla.

Tony watched like a man interested but not finally, vitally concerned. He watched La Pascualita herding the fish toward him. He watched her pounce, and he watched as she filled her pockets gleefully with the prey. But all his watching was superbly, coolly apart, there in the sanctuary of the plum trees. There wasn't much to eat in the house, but one of the unenviable facts of his life was that he no longer wanted to eat, had to remind himself to eat or pass into a state of carelessness, taking or leaving, whatever. Sometimes when Amelia called him to supper he would think what's the use, I'll be asleep before long, and then there would be breakfast, and besides if he didn't eat he would stay as firm and keen and desireable as the day he first laid eyes on her in the Fourth of July parade in Tres Rios, wearing a pastel green chiffon gown, riding in a wagon full of shining oat straw, representing the state of Ohio.

La Pascualita came to him full of evil smiles. The tails of suckers stuck out of the pockets of her down vest. They felt the air clutchingly, like villains being drawn into quicksand. She swiped the hat from his head, loaded it with fish, handed it back to him, and went for more.

Tony looked into his hat full of fish, then he folded the brim over from either side to make a lid and keep them from flopping out. This was accomplished as if he'd bought the hat for that purpose and none other, and had just been waiting for the chance to turn it into a fish basket. He gazed sadly at the work of his own hands. Once or twice, he couldn't help peeking under the brim to see what it was he held, just the carnal parts or the souls as well, which cannot be contained by any ordinary vessel.

La Pascualita came with others and others until his hat was even fuller than it had been, and then she came with seven more.

The crows watched as he gutted the suckers in the ditch. There were more of them now, and in their imperious crowlike boredom, they waited in the branches of the cottonwoods, picking lice out of their feathers and stretching their wings. By the time he reached the back porch, they were already into their nastiness. They swarmed over the discarded bowels, which to them seemed the greatest delicacies. They drew their beaks against one another, and they called each other the worst names they could think of.

Inside, La Pascualita was inspecting the dinnerware. She had all of Amelia's company plates out on the counter, and was going through the forks. She held each one in turn to the light, raised a suspicious eyebrow, and put it back down.

"Sit," she told him, taking the bucket. And he did. The table was covered with the white linen tablecloth that had not been out of the cedar chest since Tony Alire the Younger had married the Bustos girl and moved to godforsaken Denver. Everything too good to use was kept in Amelia's cedar chest, where the worms could not penetrate. It held all the hopes of her maidenhood, the sacred furnishings of marriage and the fullness that was childbirth. No man had ever looked in it, much less run his rough hands over its treasures. Not even the Sacacorcheños who'd broken in and stolen Tony's chainsaw while he and Amelia were in Nuevo Laredo, leaving the house ransacked and unclean, could bring themselves to defile it. To do so, everybody knew, would be to bring the curses of all womankind down on their heads. After all, a chain saw could be covered by insurance, but the contents of the cedar chest were an oath.

La Pascualita struggled with the cast iron skillet. She had the handle gripped fiercely in her two little bird's hands, and was trying to heave it up on top of the stove.

"Let me help," said Tony, and placed it squarely on the flame, the handle pointing west, the direction Amelia would have wanted it to face.

La Pascualita spun it around north by northeast. Then she was all energy and purpose. She cut the suckers lengthwise, speaking consolingly to each one as she massaged it in the flour. She battled her way through the spice rack. She set the table for five, and sent Tony to drag in the missing chairs from the porch. She took the three flowers from her hair and placed them in a jelly jar. She turned the suckers with her fingers, seizing them by their tails, scolding the ones who were reluctant to turn over, and giving lascivious groans of pleasure when they were brown. There was no shame in La Pascualita. She had returned from her elopement missing the sense of it, crumpled up with a load of apple crates in a boxcar of the Denver and Rio Grande; so that now, owning nothing, she was privileged to behave as if everything were hers.

While the fish cooked, she strolled around the kitchen, touching. She touched the curtains, which almost anyone but La Pascualita would have thought were as tidy as they could be. She touched the Mixmaster and the yellow pages, the dishrag and the sponge, and having touched, purified herself of every item, brushing herself off, as if there could have been anything the least bit unsavory in Amelia's kitchen. She touched him, too, but with no more gentleness than she had touched the other things. La Pascualita pinched his calves and prodded his thighs as if he, the man of the house and the provider of all that she surveyed, were just another piece of crockery.

"Don Antonio," she said, returning to pester the supper, "you are too thin."

A wonderful smell filled the house, and in spite of himself, Tony began to feel hungry. It was the kind of hunger he had not felt since his camping days, when he and little Tony would go fishing in the Rio Brazos, high up where the trout had not learned to be wary of men and their sons, where the streams were much too swift to harbor suckers. With gladness, he remembered Antonio's first fish — the fingerling — so longed for and yet so terrifying to the little boy when it finally lay there gasping in the sand; the one wide eye that looked as if it would burst from its head. He cried when Tony threw it back, and kept asking, "Is it going to die? Is it going to die, daddy?"

He felt that kind of hunger — the kind that comes from going out of doors to find your sustenance, and of breathing the heady thin air. It was the kind of hunger that gives thanks for the plainest fare and the simplest preparation; acknowledges the food, but its source, as well — the old alchemies of sun, and earth, and fish-engendering flood. Tony had not felt this hungry in years. It was the hunger of his lost and savage youth.

"Come," said La Pascualita, even though he was already there, and waiting.

Her companion spirits came down from the cupboards, where they'd been taking an afternoon snooze, and gathered around the table. When they finally stopped their fidgeting, and a look of wifely disgust told Tony to remove his hat (which would never be the same from that day forward), La Pascualita raised her hands over her head, closed her eyes, and offered thanks for the good things that had been provided.

Then they all sat down and ate the finest fish that they had ever eaten. Better, even, than trout.

TOM IRELAND grew up in New York City, studied at Harvard and Stanford, and moved to New Mexico in 1971. Lama Foundation published his journals, *Invisible Worm* (with Alyosha Zim and John McClellan) and *Mostly Mules,* an account of a journey by mule through the Southwest. From 1976 to 1983 he lived near the village of La Madera in northern New Mexico, where he built a house, raised sheep, and wrote. He holds an M.A. in creative writing from Stanford and has worked as an animal trainer, builder, artist-in-residence, and book editor. He currently lives in Santa Fe with his daughter, Hannah.

ANGIE COLEMAN grew up in Chicago. She lives with her husband and four children in Taos, New Mexico, which has been her home for the past 20 years. She has concentrated since 1985 on woodblock printing, a medium she finds well suited to the roughness of the northern New Mexico landscape.

Birds of Sorrow was output in
11½ point Garamond No. 49 at Type for U,
Cambridge, Massachusetts.

Printed in the United States of America
by Walsworth Publishing Company.